Research
Made Easy

Research
Made Easy

Classic Edition

Richard Boateng

Research Made Easy
Classic Edition

This classic edition includes teaching videos for each chapter of the book.

Author:
RICHARD BOATENG
Email: richard@pearlrichards.org

CreateSpace Independent Publishing Platform
Charleston, USA.
eStore address (i.e. www.CreateSpace.com/6440494)
Printed by CreateSpace, An Amazon.com Company
CreateSpace, Charleston SC

ISBN: 1535425512
ISBN 13: 9781535425513

To God Be The Glory
Just By Your Grace

To My Wife and Daughter
You Mean The World To Me

Table of Contents

List of Exhibits ·xi

List of Pictures · xv

Preface and Acknowledgments· xvii

Chapter 1   Why Do Research? · 1

         Objectives · 1

         What is Research? · 2

         The Research Process· 5

         Types of Research · 8

         Summary · 13

         Chapter Discussions· 14

Chapter 2   Selecting A Research Topic· 15

         Objectives · 15

         What Can Be Researched · 16

         What can Influence Choice of a Research Topic · · · · · · · · · · · · 18

         Defining Research Gaps · 20

         Identifying Gaps· 28

         Linking the Research Gaps to the Research Topic · · · · · · · · · · · 31

         Summary · 33

         Chapter Discussions· 34

Chapter 3   Reviewing The Past to Determine The Future· · · · · · · · · · · · · · · · 36

         Objectives · 36

         Literature Review Defined · 37

         Why Do Literature Review · 41

         Steps in Literature Review · 43

Categorizing Literature · 57

Analyzing and Writing· 76

Structuring a Literature Review As a Chapter/Paper · · · · · · · · · · · · 84

Summary · 87

Chapter Discussions· 88

Chapter 4   Literature Referencing · 90

Objectives · 90

Literature Referencing· 91

APA Rules for In-text Referencing · 92

Harvard Rules for In-text Referencing · 94

Producing a List of References · 96

Producing a list of references in the APA style · · · · · · · · · · · · · · · 100

How to Use Microsoft Word for Referencing · · · · · · · · · · · · · · · · · 103

Summary · 107

Chapter Discussions· 108

Chapter 5   Theory in research· 110

Objectives · 110

What is a Theory? · 111

Purpose or Goal of Theory· 113

Components of a Theory· 115

Attributes of a Good Theory · 118

Classification of Theory · 120

Schematic Representation of Theories and

Conceptual Frameworks· 125

Summary · 132

Chapter Discussions· 133

Chapter 6   Research Methodology · 134

Objectives · 134

Qualitative and Quantitative Research Explained· · · · · · · · · · · · · · 135

Key Features of Qualitative Research · 137

Types of Qualitative Research· 140

Sampling in Qualitative Research · 154

Structuring the Methodology Section of a Research

Paper and Dissertation · 157

		Summary	168
		Chapter Discussion	169
Chapter 7		Qualitative Data analysis	170
		Objectives	170
		Qualitative Data Analysis	171
		Miles and Huberman Data Analysis Approach	172
		Yin's Data Analysis Approach	183
		Argumentation: Writing and Presenting Arguments	187
		Summary	196
		Chapter Discussions	197
Chapter 8		Writing up Research	198
		Objectives	198
		Writing a Research Proposal	199
		Components of a Research Proposal	202
		Research Proposal Outline with Word Count as a Guideline	214
		Writing a Research Paper	216
		Summary	223

Appendices · 225
    Appendix A: Brief Notes on Survey · 226
    Appendix B: Glossary of "Validity and Reliability" Concepts
    in Qualitative Research · 230
    Appendix C: Philosophical Assumptions in Research · · · · · · · · · · · 235
An Example of a Research Proposal · 239
    User's Perceptions and Acceptance towards Enterprise
    Systems in Ghana · 239
    Common Errors in Submitted Dissertations · · · · · · · · · · · · · · · · · · 248
    Practice Questions · 251
Works Cited · 257
Author Profile · 265
Index · 267

List of Exhibits

Exhibit 1   Research Defined · 2

Exhibit 2   Research Significance · 4

Exhibit 3   Factors which influence choice of a research topic · · · · · · · · · · · · · · · · · 18

Exhibit 4   Social Networking in the Public Sector in Mexico · · · · · · · · · · · · · · · · · · · 29

Exhibit 5   Descriptive and Analytical Reviews · 39

Exhibit 6   Searching for Journal Articles · 49

Exhibit 7   Advanced Search for Journal Articles in Emerald Insight Database · · · · 51

Exhibit 8   One Page Summary of an Article · 54

Exhibit 9   Spider Diagram or Mind map · 56

Exhibit 10   Categorizing Literature · 57

Exhibit 11   Distribution of E-commerce in DCs Research Articles by Themes · · · · · 58

Exhibit 12   Distribution of E-commerce in DCs Research Articles by Sub-Themes · · · · 58

Exhibit 13   Distribution of E-commerce in DCs Research Articles by Year · · · · · · · · 60

Exhibit 14   Distribution of E-commerce in DCs Research Articles by Theory · · · · · 61

Exhibit 15   Mapping M-finance Research by Conceptual and Methodological
Approaches · 62

Exhibit 16   Mapping conceptual approaches to m-finance research in DCs · · · · · · · 63

Exhibit 17   Distributions of E-commerce in DCs Articles by Research Methods · · · 65

Exhibit 18   Mapping of M-finance Research Themes by Level of Analysis · · · · · · · · 66

Exhibit 19   Distributions of E-commerce in DCs Articles by Region from
1993-2005 · 68

Exhibit 20   Distribution of E-commerce in DCs Articles by Selected Journals · · · · · 71

Exhibit 21   Number of Articles by Infrastructure · 72

Exhibit 22   Research Gaps in E-commerce in DCs Research · · · · · · · · · · · · · · · · · · · 74

Exhibit 23   Social Networking in the Workplace · 78

Exhibit 24   Sample Outlines of A Literature Review (Non-Research
              Graduate Student)······································84
Exhibit 25   Outline of A Detailed Literature Review (Research Graduate Student) ····85
Exhibit 26   Gregor's Components of a Theory·································117
Exhibit 27   Example of a Cause and Effect Model ····························125
Exhibit 28   Example of a Process-based Model ····························126
Exhibit 29   Example of a Hierarchy-based Framework ·························127
Exhibit 30   Example of a Gap-based Framework·····························128
Exhibit 31   Example of a Map-based Framework ·····························129
Exhibit 32   Example of a Force-Field Diagram ····························130
Exhibit 33   Comparison of Quantitative and Qualitative Research Approaches ·····136
Exhibit 34   Characteristics of Four Types of Qualitative Research ··············141
Exhibit 35   Research Methodology - Example 1 ····························160
Exhibit 36   Research Methodology - Example 2 ····························161
Exhibit 37   Research Methodology - Example 3 ····························163
Exhibit 38   Flow Model of Qualitative Data Analysis Components ·············171
Exhibit 39   Miles and Huberman's Data Analysis Approach·····················172
Exhibit 40   Contact Summary Template ····································173
Exhibit 41   An Example of Coding Reponses ·····························176
Exhibit 42   An Example of Memoing·······································177
Exhibit 43   An Example of Data Display Using Process Diagram·················179
Exhibit 44   An Example of Data Display Using a Table for Comparison ··········180
Exhibit 45   Tactics for Conclusion Drawing and Verification ····················181
Exhibit 46   Example of Conclusion Drawing and Verifying·····················182
Exhibit 47   Example of Cross-Case Syntheses·····························185
Exhibit 48   Example of Arguing Evidentially·································188
Exhibit 49   Example of Arguing Interpretively or Narratively·····················189
Exhibit 50   An Example of Arguing Reflexively or Multivocally··················190
Exhibit 51   An Example of Arguing Evocatively or Illustratively ·················190
Exhibit 52   An Example of Theoretical Generalization·························193
Exhibit 53   Extracts from Schutt on Computer-assisted Qualitative Data Analysis ··194
Exhibit 54   Outline of Research Proposal and Chapter One of Dissertation······200
Exhibit 55   An example of a Research Background ····························202

Exhibit 56   An example of a Research Problem · 203
Exhibit 57   An example of Significance of Research · 206
Exhibit 58   An example of Significance of Research · 208
Exhibit 59   An example of a Research Methodology · 209
Exhibit 60   An example of Research Limitations and Delimitations · · · · · · · · · · · · · 210
Exhibit 61   An example of a Research Project Schedule · 212
Exhibit 62   An example of a Chapter Outline · 212
Exhibit 63   Examples of Abstracts · 217
Exhibit 64   Research Paradigms · 236

List of Pictures

Picture 1   Literature Review Snapshot · 79
Picture 2   Referencing with MS Word 2010 – Step 1 · 103
Picture 3   Referencing with MS Word 2010 – Step 2 · 104
Picture 4   Referencing with MS Word 2010 – Step 3 · 104
Picture 5   Referencing with MS Word 2010 – Step 4 · 105
Picture 6   Referencing with MS Word 2010 – Step 5 · 105
Picture 7   Referencing with MS Word 2010 – Step 6 · 106

Preface and Acknowledgments

YOU ARE WELCOME to Research Made Easy. I put this book together as a guide for researchers and students carrying out a research project or working on long essays, theses and dissertations. The book is a companion for conducting and writing out research.

What are the elements of a good research? Most often than not we face a dilemma in seeking answers to this question. The challenge becomes pronounced when we begin to evaluate the different requirements of the diverse academic audiences in the social sciences and business. So what really makes a good research? In this book, I attempt to provide a general outline which can be considered as being essential for a good research thesis. Though this is not exhaustive, it will be of help, especially to young researchers. The purpose is not to create a 'one best format', but to offer guidelines in starting a research project and the preparation of long essays, theses and dissertations for submission.

This book is essential for anyone involved in business and social science studies. On completion, the reader would have acquired practical research skills to select a research topic, review literature, identify research gaps, conceptualize research designs, and conduct data collection and analysis to address research gaps.

Many people contributed to this book both directly and indirectly, and I would like to thank them for their support and patience. First, my profound gratitude goes to my friends and advisors, Prof. Richard Heeks (University of Manchester) and Prof. Alemayehu Molla (RMIT University) for their patient mentoring and supervision, which made the writing of this book challenging and a real learning experience.

Second, special thanks to Prof. Victor Mbarika, Southern University A&M, Baton Rouge, USA and senior faculty of the University of Ghana, Prof. Joshua Abor, Prof. Robert Hinson, Dr. John Effah, Dr. Francis Banuro, and Dr. Charles Andoh, for their enormous assistance and direction they gave me during the teaching of research methods. To the research students, Mr. Joseph Budu, Mr. Augustus Anderson, Mr. Eric Ansong, Mr. Bernard Okyere, Mr. Stephen Boateng, Mr. Anthony Mensah, and Mr. Prince Senyo of the University of Ghana, and Mr. Isaac Jackson of PearlRichards Foundation, I express my gratitude for coordinating research activities which were used as case examples in this book.

Last but definitely not least, many thanks to my wife, Sheena Lovia Boateng, for her understanding, motivation and support during my long nights at the computer. She is the inspiration for my writing and my life. Because of her, as wife, supporter, and detailed and careful editor, this work has been made possible. And also to the inspiration of the family, Astrid Nhyira Boateng, your mum and dad, adore you so much and we say thank you for your smile, which keeps us through each day.

CHAPTER 1

Why Do Research?

Objectives

This chapter seeks to introduce readers to the purpose of research and explains the research process. The learning outcome is to understand what is and what is not research, understand the classifications or different types of research and explain what a research design is.

What is Research?

RESEARCH IS AN investigation into a particular topic or social/business phenomenon. That said, one may argue that every investigation on a topic of interest is research. NO! That is not true. Most often than not, every activity which involves the search for information or answers to questions is christened as research. However, research like a number of other social or scientific activities has principles or guidelines.

In academia or scholarly circles, research is an investigation into a particular topic or social/business phenomenon using scientific principles and methods; and also drawing on a variety of reliable, scholarly resources. Since research relies on scientific principles it tends to be systematic and also fairly organized (see Exhibit 1). Research is an "organized and systematic way of finding answers to questions" [HYPERLINK \l "Hen97" 1]. It is not just about talking and asking questions.

EXHIBIT 1 RESEARCH DEFINED

Research is an ORGANIZED and SYSTEMATIC way of FINDING ANSWERS to QUESTIONS.

1. **SYSTEMATIC** because there is a definite set of scientific procedures and principles which the researcher will NEED to follow in order to get reliable and accurate results.
2. **ORGANIZED** because there is a structure or method for doing research. The research process has a number of steps to guide the researcher.
3. **FINDING ANSWERS** because every research seeks to answer a question or a number of questions. Sometimes the answer is no, but it is still an answer.
4. **QUESTIONS** are central to research. If there is no question, then how do we begin the research? Research is focused on relevant, useful, and important questions. Without a question, research has no focus, drive, or purpose.

Adapted from [1]

SO WHY DO WE DO RESEARCH?

We do research to DISCOVER/EXPLORE, UNDERSTAND, DESCRIBE, EXPLAIN and/or PREDICT/CREATE social or scientific phenomena. Through this process we may create and develop new knowledge or products, explain or attempt to make sense of what is happening and/or identify patterns which enable us to predict a particular social or scientific phenomenon. Through research we may also analyze information, establish facts and propose or arrive at new conclusions concerning a particular topic or social or business phenomenon. Research is partly a process of discovery and partly a process of knowledge creation.

THE ABSENCE OF RESEARCH

Without research the common sources of perception, information and knowledge tend to be authority, tradition, common sense, media distortion/myth and personal experience [2]. Most of what we know is learnt through these alternatives to research. Authority means accepting something as true or as a fact because it comes from a person of authority. For example, when a manager gives business information to an employee, the employee is likely to accept it because the manager has higher authority. Tradition refers to accepting something as true or as a fact because it is based on the past – passed on from previous generations and has now become a norm or the way it has always been. Such knowledge or information may even be distorted or prejudiced. Common sense refers to ordinary reasoning which may be built from a person's experiences and sometimes tradition. Common sense sometimes contains errors or may be prejudiced. Media myth refers to arriving at conclusions based on a reality created by the media. Often media can create a reality which is inaccurate but has a purpose to entertain. Personal experience refers to learning through our sensory impressions and knowledge – 'seeing is believing'. However, personal experiences are also often biased, prejudiced or inaccurate because of over-generalization (extending the truth to inapplicable events), selective observation (stemming from biases or preconceptions), premature closure (concluding on incomplete information) and the halo effect (over-generalization based on the positive).

The author, Neuman [2] notes that social research involves a set of processes to create new knowledge that is based on science. As such, we move away from learning by authority, tradition, common sense, media distortion/myth and personal experience. These rigorous processes are defined by the scientific community as the research principles to create new knowledge or find answers to questions in a manner that is accurate, reliable and less prone to error. We rather make a choice for using scientific principles to carry out research or seek answers on questions about social phenomena.

WHO NEEDS RESEARCH?

Exhibit 2 showcases an example of the potential significance of a research on electronic banking in rural banks.

EXHIBIT 2 RESEARCH SIGNIFICANCE

Topic: Electronic Banking in Rural Banks

The significance of the study can be viewed along three strands: research, practice and policy. Concerning the research significance, this study goes beyond current research on e-banking in rural banks by examining the strategies for implementing and integrating e-banking technologies. Literature on the strategic perspective of e-banking in rural banks is arguably non-existent on Ghana and perhaps this spreads to the West-African region.

Concerning significance to practice, the study will provide guidelines to other rural banks on the factors which influence e-banking adoption and strategic options to address challenges in managing and sustaining e-banking applications. This will be very helpful to ARB Apex Bank and to rural banks in its network.

Concerning significance to policy, the study will provide feedback on policies driving the computerization of rural banks which is critical to the operations of the financier, the Millennium Challenge Corporation, the government of Ghana and other donors who have an interest in supporting ICT integration in rural banks. These contributions to practice and policy will become necessary to the development of more advanced or complex functionalities for rural banks including internet banking and mobile banking.

Research feeds into future research, practice and policy. Thus, research is needed by researchers, practitioners and policy makers. In these broad categories, there are a number of stakeholders including organizations, communities, government and non-governmental institutions and society in general. Research has to feed into a body of knowledge or practice or policy. Without a connection to any of these, the readers and reviewers will ask "And so what?" meaning what can we do with your findings and what are its implications?

The Research Process

As mentioned in the previous section, research involves a number of steps which need to be followed. The research process is the step by step process of creating and carrying out a research project. It involves the steps or activities in the entire investigative process of identifying a social phenomenon to be studied, determining the right question to ask, finding answers and informing others about the answers to the questions. The steps in the research process can be outlined as:

1. Selecting a Topic – Research Topic
2. Determining the Question – Research Question
3. Reviewing Literature – Literature Review
4. Designing the Research – Research Design
5. Collecting Data – Research Data Collection
6. Analyzing and Interpreting Data – Research Analysis and Conclusion
7. Informing Others – Research Write Up and Publishing

Some other authors and literature provide a detailed outline which is between eight to 12 steps [3]. For example, a detailed research process may be conceptualized as follows:

1. Selecting a Topic – Research Topic
2. Determining the Problem (Preliminary Literature Review) – Research Problem
3. Determining Research Gaps – Research Gaps
4. Determining the Hypotheses (Preliminary Literature Review) – Research Hypotheses[1]
5. Determining the Objectives – Research Objectives
6. Determining the Question – Research Question
7. Detailed Review of Literature – Literature Review
8. Determining Research Framework – Research Framework (including hypotheses)
9. Designing the Research – Research Design
10. Collecting Data – Research Data Collection
11. Analyzing and Interpreting Data – Research Analysis and Conclusion
12. Informing Others – Research Write Up and Publishing

---

1 Not every research requires hypotheses.

The detailed research process outlines all the key components needed to carry out a research. This book covers all the twelve steps outlined in the research process. Despite the type of research process (simple or detailed) a researcher seeks to follow, the researcher has to understand some key principles about the research process.

PRINCIPLE 1: PHASES OF RESEARCH PROCESS

Every research needs four key phases of activities, namely:

- **Phase 1:** Identify a social or business phenomenon to be studied;
- **Phase 2:** Determine the right question to ask;
- **Phase 3:** Design a research to find answers; and
- **Phase 4:** Inform others about the answers to the question or new knowledge.

Thus the twelve activities in the research processes can be summarized into the four phases outlined above. Each phase is critical to achieving answers which are reliable, accurate and less prone to error. It is also important to know that, the research process as used in this book is different from the concept of research process as used in libraries [4]. For most libraries, research process refers to the means of effectively locating information for a research project; be it a research paper, an oral presentation, or something else assigned by a lecturer to a student [5]. That type of research process is more about locating or searching for literature to conduct a review in an assignment. Its' process is different from the systematic investigation or inquiry that is designed to collect, analyze, interpret, and use data to understand, describe, or predict a social or business phenomenon.

PRINCIPLE 2: RESEARCH PROCESS IS NOT RESEARCH DESIGN

Research design is often confused to be same as the research process. The two research activities are different. The researcher's plan on how to implement the research in practice is known as the research design [6]. The research design describes how, when and where data is to be collected and how the data will be analyzed. The plan also covers how the researcher will identify a research sample, address the ethical issues in data collection, ensure the internal and external validity of the study, analyze results and disseminate results [7].

So before a researcher can develop a research design, the researcher needs to be sure about the social or business phenomenon to be studied and the right question to ask. Identifying the phenomenon to be studied and determining the right question to ask is part of the research process and not part of the research design. The research design is rather a subset of the research process (see the outline of research process above). The research design provides structure and direction to the research process after the research problem, objectives, questions and framework have been determined.

PRINCIPLE 3: RESEARCH ACTIVITIES ARE OFTEN ITERATIVE

The research activities within the research process are often iterative. For example, after the preliminary literature review, a researcher may realize the research topic is too narrow or well-researched; hence there may be a need to change the research topic and redefine the research problem. In other scenarios, the researcher may even change the research questions and objectives after a preliminary visit or pilot study of the research site where data will be collected. As a result, the research activities in a research process are not on a linear path but more of a cyclical path. The research also has the flexibility of revisiting previous activities to revise their focus. Mertens [8] echoes this point arguing that the "research process is rarely linear; it is more realistically cyclical with the researcher returning to earlier steps, while at the same time moving ahead to later steps" (cited in [9]).

As of now, we understand what research is and can outline the research process; the next section will explain the types of research.

Types of Research

There are a number of criteria which can be used to categorize the various types of research. In this book we will discuss how research differs according to the following:

1. Application of the Research or Use of the Research Results
2. Purpose or Objectives of the Research
3. Inquiry Procedure of the Research
   a. Paradigm or Philosophies underpinning the Research
   b. Approach of the research
   c. Time dimension of the research

APPLICATION OF THE RESEARCH

Depending on how the research results are going to be used, research can be classified as being either basic or applied research [2]. Basic research, also known as pure research refers to a type of research which seeks to serve the scientific community. The results or knowledge is supposed to contribute to the existing body of knowledge. In pure research, the audience is the research community and hence, there is more focus on the rigor of the research design. Success is achieved through acceptance by the scientific community and perhaps, publication in refereed academic journals. On the other hand, applied research has a more practical focus. The results or knowledge is supposed to contribute to practitioner knowledge and policy formulation and development.

In applied research, the audience is normally outside the scientific community and hence, there is more focus on how findings or results contribute to the interests of the company or agency funding the research. Success is achieved through the application of the results or findings by the funding agency or other stakeholders. Applied research may either be exploratory to understand a phenomenon, or assess or evaluate a potential social impact of an intended activity. For example, an applied research may seek to assess the potential impact of constructing a road through the market in a town. Hence, the question is: What will be the potential impact of the road to be constructed through the town's market?

PURPOSE OR OBJECTIVES OF THE RESEARCH

Depending on the purpose of the research, research can be classified as exploratory, descriptive explanatory or correlational. Exploratory research seeks to explore an area where little is known or little research has been done either in the context (research site) or on the research topic in that particular context (topic and context). For example, in one of my co-authored papers we explored the prospects of m-commerce adoption in Ghana. The paper was titled 'Preliminary insights into m-commerce adoption in Ghana'. At the time of conducting the research, there was barely any previous research on mobile commerce or even mobile business in Ghana. Hence, our research was one of the first of its kind. Through exploratory research, a researcher may obtain more knowledge concerning an unknown or poorly-understood phenomenon and pose more research gaps or more questions for future research.

Descriptive research seeks to systematically describe a phenomenon, situation or problem. Descriptive research usually asks the 'what' question. For example, what are the attitudes of the community towards the community library or what are the living conditions in the farming communities in Ghana? Explanatory research seeks to understand and explain a phenomenon, situation or problem. In order to explain, explanatory research usually asks the questions 'why' and 'how' a particular phenomenon occurs or there exists a relationship between two or more factors of a phenomenon. For example, why and how do firms achieve value amidst the reported fierce competition in the micro-finance industry? Correlational research seeks to discover or establish the existence of a relationship between two or more factors or aspects of a phenomenon. For example, a correlational research may seek to find out whether the grade a student receives depends upon the number of hours the student will study.

INQUIRY PROCEDURE OF THE RESEARCH

The inquiry procedure can also differentiate research in a number of ways, namely the research philosophies or paradigms, approach of the research and the time dimension of the research.

Research Philosophies and Paradigm

A paradigm is "a set of beliefs, values and techniques which is shared by members of a scientific community, and which acts as a guide or map, dictating the kinds of problems scientists should address and the types of explanations that are acceptable to them" [10]. Paradigms, as a set of beliefs, values and techniques, which form the fundamental philosophical assumptions which define what 'valid' research is and the appropriate methods that can be applied in that research [11]. As various taxonomies exist to distinguish paradigms, there also exist various and diverse paradigms. The most commonly referred or dominant paradigms that reflect the major theoretical directions in social science research are positivism, interpretivist, realism, relativism and critical realism [12,13,14,11,15,16]. Hence, research can be categorized according to these paradigms. These paradigms are discussed in Appendix C.

Approach of the Research

Researchers have the option of making a choice between three research approaches:

- **Quantitative or Structured Approach:** Quantitative research seeks to determine the extent of a problem or the existence of a relationship between aspects of a phenomenon by quantifying the variation. Quantitative research often seeks to test to support or disprove a proposed relationship between two or more aspects of a phenomenon. For example, a researcher may ask, 'to what extent have students adopted mobile phones?' Quantitative research is structured because it starts with specific hypotheses or questions derived from theory/previous research and uses objective instruments (e.g. fixed choice questionnaires, attitude scales, etc.) to collect data from a selected sample. The results are presented using statistics and inferences made to the population. Throughout this process, the researcher is viewed as being independent from subjects involved in the research. Hence, there is a "distance" between the researcher and the subjects and an emphasis on following the research design.
- **Qualitative or Unstructured Approach:** Qualitative research tends to explore the meanings, attitudes, values, beliefs people associate with a phenomenon in order to establish a better understanding, rather than to test

to support or disprove a relationship. This approach is useful for describing the nature of a problem, issue, situation or phenomenon. For example, a researcher may ask, 'What are the working conditions in the banking industry'? Qualitative research is arguably unstructured as it starts with general research problems and not by formulating hypotheses (hypotheses may emerge from the data analysis). It uses relatively unstructured instruments (e.g. interviews, observations, etc.) and "intense" data collection (e.g. over extended periods of time). Data is collected from a small, purposive sample (not random) which may or may not be representative of the larger population. The results are presented mainly or exclusively in words. It is more about explanation, and de-emphasizing generalizations to the population. Throughout this process, the researcher is aware of his/her own orientations, biases or experiences and personal interaction with subjects or the context of the study. The qualitative approach allows flexibility in all activities of the research process.

- **Mixed Methods (Quantitative and Qualitative) Approach:** Both qualitative and quantitative research approaches have their strengths and weaknesses. Mixed-methods approach tends to combine the strengths of both the qualitative and quantitative approaches to conduct a research. Some studies require the researcher to combine both approaches. For example, suppose a researcher wants to find the type of primary schools in the city of Accra and the extent of their popularity in the city. The type of primary schools is the qualitative aspect of the study since it entails the description of school and the educational culture. The extent of popularity is the quantitative aspect as it involves estimating the number of applications for admissions and calculating the other indicators that reflect the extent of popularity.

TIME DIMENSION OF THE RESEARCH

Time influences research in the manner in which data is collected with respect to time. Hence, the number of different types of research, namely:

- **Cross-sectional Study:** A researcher collects information from a sample drawn from a population. The data the researcher obtains is derived from a cross-section of the population at one point in time. An example is a survey on consumer perceptions of internet banking services.

- **Longitudinal Study:** There are two types of longitudinal studies – Panel and Cohort Study. In Panel studies, a researcher can identify a sample from the beginning and follow the specific respondents over a specified period of time to observe changes in specific respondents and highlight the reasons why these respondents have changed. As a result, the researcher observes the exact same people at two or more times. For example, a researcher may choose to study a particular group of students at two or more times. Each time the exact same students are involved in the research. In Cohort studies, the researcher observes people who shared an experience at two or more times. Although the population remains the same, different respondents are sampled each time. The researcher's aim here is to see if there are changes in perceptions or trends that occur in the study.

- **Time-series Study:** A research design in which selected aspects (variables) of a phenomenon is studied at different points in time, often with a view to studying social trends. For this reason such studies are also known as trend studies (or designs). Time series research may sometimes utilize official data; For example, a researcher studying crime rates may plot crime rates for the same area but for different points in time (monthly, quarterly, annually) [17]. The result will provide information on trends in the levels of crime.

Summary

In this chapter, we explained the concept of research. Research was defined as an organized and systematic way of finding answers to questions. In academia or scholarly circles, research is an investigation into a particular topic or social/business phenomenon using scientific principles and methods and also drawing on a variety of reliable, scholarly resources. Without research the common sources of perception, information and knowledge tend to be authority, tradition, common sense, media distortion/myth and personal experience.

We also learnt about the research process as the steps required for undertaking the research. The research process has four phases: Phase 1: Identify a social or business phenomenon to be studied; Phase 2: Determine the right question to ask; Phase 3: Design a research to find answers; and Phase 4: Inform others about the answers to the question or new knowledge. The research process is rarely linear; it is more realistically cyclical and iterative.

Finally, we also learnt about the types of research. Research differs according to the following: application of the research; purpose of the research and the inquiry procedure of the research. Concerning the application of the research, research can either be pure (basic) or applied. Concerning the purpose of research, research can be exploratory, descriptive, explanatory or correlational. Concerning the inquiry procedure, the research can differ by research paradigms, research approach (quantitative, qualitative and mixed-methods) and time dimension of the research.

In the next chapter we will begin to explore the activities of the research process by discussing how to select a research topic.

Chapter Discussions

QUESTION 1
On Monday, a journalist from Radio Universe, a radio station on the University of Ghana Campus, interviewed 10 people randomly chosen on the streets of the university campus concerning the state of the Ghanaian economy. Six of the interviews were played on radio as part of their evening news bulletin. From your understanding of research, do you think Radio Universe conducted a research?

QUESTION 2
In the absence of research, the common sources of perception, information and knowledge tend to be authority, tradition, common sense, media distortion/myth and personal experience. Discuss the implications of such sources of knowledge in an endeavor to improve society.

QUESTION 3
In the absence of research, the common sources of information and knowledge tend to be authority, tradition, common sense, media distortion/myth and personal experience. Discuss the implications of such sources of knowledge in an endeavor to improve society and advance knowledge.

QUESTION 4
The centrality of every research is the question being asked. Discuss.

CHAPTER 2

Selecting A Research Topic

Objectives

This chapter seeks to discuss how to select a research topic. The learning outcome is to understand what is and what is not researchable, understand the characteristics of a good research topic and how to frame a concise and brief research topic.

What Can Be Researched

THE TOPIC OR area of research a student chooses to write on can either make or break a research project. Hence, it is imperative that the student choose the right topic to conduct a research on, and be aware of what topics to avoid. Some areas to be avoided include: common/over-used topics, topics related to religion/controversy, and general/broad topics.

COMMON/OVER-USED TOPICS

A number of research areas are very common, and have been reused several times by numerous other students. Readers need fresh material to keep them engaged and interested in the research while reading. Therefore topic recycling must be avoided at all cost, even if it is a topic that the researcher has a strong interest in. Most importantly, try to be original. You can pick an over-used topic but you can place it in another context or sector. For example, if internet banking in Ghana has been well-researched, you may consider a topic on internet banking among rural banks in Ghana. This is likely to bring in a fresh or new perspective, since rural and community banks are less discussed in academic literature on Africa.

TOPICS RELATED TO RELIGION/CONTROVERSY

Topics related to religion and controversies have the propensity to arouse emotions in people, usually because the surrounding issues are highly subjective. Even if the researcher has good intentions for undertaking the project, some parties could take offence at the content and findings. Hence, such topics must be avoided, unless the program of study necessitates a religious viewpoint or otherwise.

GENERAL/ BROAD TOPICS

Some topics are too broad and general in scope, and thus should be avoided. Students must learn to tweak their choice of topic in order to narrow down their focus and specific zone of interest. For instance, to conduct a research on e-commerce, the topic can be narrowed down to e-commerce in Ghana or e-commerce in the fashion industry in Ghana.

TOPICS THAT ARE TOO NARROW

Picking a topic that is too narrow should be avoided, because it will be near impossible to find enough information to conduct the research. For example, consider the research topic 'why graduate students in the University of Ghana failed economics in the 2011/12 academic year' or 'Why John broke up with Sarah'. These topics are too narrow and focused on a single event. It seems to be more of an investigation about a particular event instead of a topic which is more general and contribute some knowledge to literature or policy and practice. However, if these topics are changed to: 'Factors which influence students' performance in economic subjects' or 'Determinants of break-ups in relationships among undergraduate students' – the topics will become more researchable.

POLITICS RELATED TOPICS

Topics directly linked to politics need to be shunned unless you are a researcher of political science. This is mainly because there is no simple way to discuss politics without stepping on a few toes or taking a firm definitive perspective. More so because there is no way of knowing the viewpoints of your audience concerning the topic you are researching.

These are, however, not set in stone. The researcher can make sound and logical arguments supported by research and data, while writing on any one of these areas. When this is done, the final reader should be able to appreciate the accuracy and validity of the research, even if they don't necessarily support the views presented by the research.

What can Influence Choice of a Research Topic

EXHIBIT 3 FACTORS WHICH INFLUENCE CHOICE OF A RESEARCH TOPIC

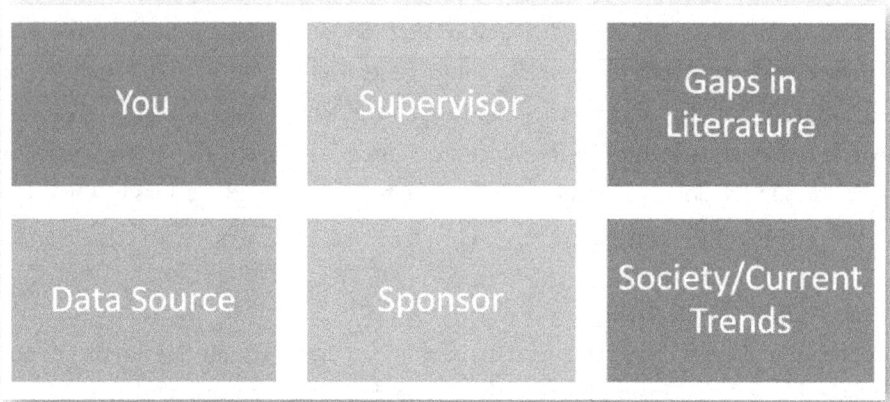

You	Supervisor	Gaps in Literature
Data Source	Sponsor	Society/Current Trends

The factors which influence the research topic can be categorized in six: You (the researcher); the research supervisor; the data source; the sponsor; the gaps in literature and the current trends (Exhibit 3). First, the researcher's values, beliefs and interests can influence their choice of a research topic. Sometimes a researcher can be curious about a topic either because of personal experience or because it has been recommended by a friend. For example, my PhD research topic was highly influenced by a term paper on electronic business which I wrote during my masters' degree. I revised the term paper into my PhD proposal.

Second, the choice of a research topic can be influenced by the potential supervisor of the research. In most universities, students are encouraged to discuss their research interests with faculty before selecting the topics. This preliminary discussion can enable the student to identify the most appropriate supervisor for the research and also make sure the interests of student are aligned with that of the supervisor. On a number of occasions, I have witnessed students struggle through their long essays and dissertations, just because of the poor interest or support of the research supervisor. Hence, my advice is for students to take the initiative and discuss their work with the faculty in their department. Supervisors usually consider such students to be serious and offer help by supervising or recommending a more appropriate member of faculty as a supervisor.

Third, the current trends and issues in society can influence the choice of the research topic. For example, current media reportage on climate change has made climate change a prominent topic among most research conferences and academic research. Thus researchers can select a topic based on how important a particular issue is perceived to be to the society at that point in time.

Fourth, researchers are sometimes restricted to particular topics because of access to or lack of access to data in the specific field of study. Even when they have access, researchers can be constrained by time. Fifth, researchers can also be restricted by the sponsor or funding agency. Most funding agencies have specific topics of interests which are based on their goals and objectives. For example, a biochemistry research funding agency is very unlikely to sponsor a research on micro-finance institutions. Funding agencies and sponsors can also influence how the findings are reported. The researcher may be required to edit the final report in order to promote the interests of the sponsor. The sponsor can also restrict the researcher in the choice of data source and time available for the study. As a result, in sponsored research, the resource requirements, in terms of finance, time and data access must be well understood early in the research process.

Sixth, a research topic may be selected from the areas of study where there are reasonable gaps in the existing research literature. This is the most recommended option for every researcher – because academic research always has to demonstrate that there is a 'gap' or an opportunity for something new or something to be questioned in existing research literature and thus, points out a potential contribution to knowledge. Research gaps also refer to the discrepancies in literature which need to be addressed or areas of study which need attention.

The next section of this chapter will explain research gaps and their role in research and in the formulation of a research problem. The learning outcome is to understand the different research gaps in social science research and how they influence future research.

Defining Research Gaps

Research gaps are the discrepancies in existing research literature which need to be addressed. They refer to the areas of study where there are reasonable gaps or as earlier mentioned, an opportunity for something new or something to be questioned in the existing literature. Research gaps enable researchers to formulate their research problems. They form a critical component of the research problem –through which the research purpose, objectives and questions emerge. Research gaps enable the researcher to answer the following questions:

- Why should others read this research paper?
- Is the researcher just duplicating previous research?
- What is the potential contribution of this research?
- Is there any value or something new to be learnt or discovered, described or explained?

Hence, the potential contribution to literature lies in the gaps in research.

TYPES OF RESEARCH GAPS

Research gaps differ in terms of the area of research where a discrepancy can be found or identified. The more dominant types of research gaps can be categorized as:

Issue Gap

- An issue which is less discussed or less represented in literature. Very little is known about this issue.

Theory Gap

- A theory or theoretical framework which is less discussed, or less represented in literature. Theory gaps can also exist when current theories or conceptual models are inadequate in addressing a particular research issue.

Method Gap

- A research method which is less discussed or less represented in literature in respect of a particular research topic/issue. Sometimes researchers make a case for new research methods or approaches to be used for a particular research issue. Inconclusive/conflicting empirical results can also create method gaps.

Context Gap

- A research context – includes sector, industry or geographic region – which is less discussed or less represented in literature, especially in respect of a particular research issue.

Level of Analysis Gap

- A level of analysis (meta, macro, meso and micro) – which is less discussed or less represented in literature, especially in respect of a particular research issue.

Research gaps are sometimes complex in their presentation, thus two or more types of research gaps may be combined to create a **Complex Research Gap**. Complex research gaps may exist as:

- Issue + Context;
- Issue + Theory;
- Issue + Method;
- Issue + Level of Analysis;
- Theory + Context; and
- Theory + Method.

Most undergraduate and graduate research work tends to focus on issue gaps and sometimes issue and context gaps. For a PhD research work, some supervisors may require students to go beyond the issue and contribute to theory or method. Gaps may be communicated as

1.   Missing issues in literature;
2.   Limited discussion in literature;
3.   Conflicts in theoretical approach;
4.   Missing theoretical model;
5.   Conflicts in empirical methods (data collection and level of analysis);
6.   Mixed previous empirical results;
7.   Less contextual evaluation or geographic representation; and
8.   Complex (limited previous results, conflicts, absence, mixed views).

Let us review a number of examples to understand the differences between the types of gaps explained above.

EXAMPLE 1: RESEARCH PROBLEM – ILLUSTRATING AN ISSUE AND CONTEXT GAP

Corporate Governance and Financing
Decisions of Ghanaian Listed Firms

Corporate governance has been identified in previous studies to influence firms' financing or capital structure decisions which also affect performance (see Berger et al., 1997; Friend and Lang, 1988). These empirical studies tended to focus mainly on developed economies with inconclusive results. Very little, however, has been done on corporate governance in Sub-Saharan Africa, especially with respect to firms' financing decisions. In Ghana for instance, economic development and restructuring have introduced modern forms of business activity and diverse financing structures like the Ghana Stock Exchange (GSE) in the past two decades (Ghana Stock Exchange, 1993).

Thus firms are being exposed to more financing options than previously. It is crucial to determine how current issues in corporate governance affect the financing decisions of Ghanaian firms. This paper specifically examines the relationship between various variables of corporate governance and the capital structure decisions of firms listed on the GSE during the six-year period (1998-2003).

Source: [18]

EXAMPLE 2: RESEARCH PROBLEM – ILLUSTRATING A CONTEXT AND ISSUE GAP

Impact of Mobile Phones on Micro-trading Activities

Extant literature has fairly covered studies on the mobile phone's usage and mobiles for development in sub-Saharan Africa. The studies include mobile phones and fisherman and farmers in Ghana (Boadi et al., 2007); mobile phone sharing practices in Ghana (Sey, 2009); mobile phones and development in Nigeria (Heeks and Jagun, 2007; Jagun et al., 2008); mobile payments in Uganda (Duncombe, 2009) and mobile phone ownership and social capital in Tanzania and South Africa (Goodman, 2005).

Despite these studies, there is a call for more studies to test earlier findings in different contexts and in different micro-economic activities in order to contribute to a better understanding of the impact of mobile phones in developing economies.

Source: [19]

EXAMPLE 3: RESEARCH PROBLEM – ILLUSTRATING AN ISSUE, LEVEL OF ANALYSIS AND CONTEXT GAP

Social Networking in the Public Sector in Mexico

The adoption of social media by the government confronts a series of barriers. Some of these barriers relate to records management, privacy and security issues, accuracy, and administration-specific requirements (Bertot et al., 2012; Bryer and Zavattaro, 2011; Landsbergen, 2010 and Sherman, 2011). As social media includes two-way communications, the risk of inserting malware into governments' websites exists (Bertot et al., 2012), so the IT people should be prepared to protect government's information technology infrastructure. Governments that would like to implement social media need to verify if people in charge of updating the media will have the time to update the new communication channel; they also need to answer other questions such as what to post, how and when often they will update (Bryer and Zavattaro, 2011 and Landsbergen, 2010). The lack of resources and procedures could undermine the accuracy of the information posted on social media.

Although the use of social media in Mexican state government portals is recent, the development of relationships between government and citizens is growing fast (Sandoval-Almazán et al., 2011). However, in contrast with other countries, to our knowledge, there is still no guideline for the use of social media in Mexico. The study of perceived risks, benefits, and strategies will be very helpful in the development of those guidelines.

Source: [20]

EXAMPLE 4: RESEARCH PROBLEM – ILLUSTRATING A MODEL/THEORY GAP

Evaluating Self-Access Language Learning Centers

In education in general, evaluation has played a vital role for more than one hundred years (Madaus et al., 1983). In English Language Teaching also, evaluation has been a major concern for over twenty years (Strevens, 1976; Stern, 1983; Lynch, 1996). In contrast, it is only recently (Star, 1994; Gardner and Miller, 1999) that attention has been paid to the evaluation of learning outcomes in self-access centers. However, if we are to argue that such centers provide an effective and efficient alternative to other existing modes of language learning, it remains a matter of serious concern that there is no research-based model designed for their evaluation.

This paper will suggest four key issues which need to be addressed when considering the development of such an evaluation model...

Source: [21]

EXAMPLE 5: RESEARCH PROBLEM – ILLUSTRATING AN ISSUE, THEORY, AND CONTEXT GAP

Resource-based Analysis of E-commerce in Developing Countries

E-commerce presents a lot of opportunities and benefits to firms in developing countries (DCs). There is some evidence of developing country firms achieving strategic, informational and operational benefits from e-commerce adoption (Moodley and Morris 2004, Molla and Heeks 2007). Despite these studies about e-commerce in DCs, there is comparatively little research conducted on how DC firms develop, deploy, and manage resources to realize e-commerce benefits. A prevailing paradigm for understanding how and why firms develop the capability to gain and sustain competitive advantage, and moreover, adapt and even capitalize on rapidly changing technological environments is the resource-based view of the firm (RBV) (Mahoney and Pandian, 1992; Schendel, 1994) and its later extension, dynamic capabilities approach (Teece et al., 1997). A survey of literature on e-commerce in DCs (Boateng et al., 2009) identified the application of these theories in only four studies: Montealegre (2002); García-Murillo (2004); Zhu and Kraemer (2005); and Cui et al. (2006). These studies highlight a number of research gaps:

- García-Murillo (2004) study pointed out that there exists a mismatch between the realities for DC firms and assumptions of Western models of enterprise (such as Porter's (1990) recommendations), thus proposing that as organizational business practices evolve with their changing business environments, more research is needed to redefine existing knowledge to be consistent and applicable with the dynamic nature of the environment.
- Montealegre (2002) also emphasizes the need for a process-based model of dynamic capability development as compared to the present existence of factor-oriented models which fail to offer understanding of how these capabilities are developed, deployed and managed in alignment with a firm's overall strategy. Future research could offer such understanding by developing a process-based model of resource or dynamic capability development.
- Cui et al. (2006) suggest that IT management, compared with IT infrastructure, plays a more important role in foreign invested firms than that in local and joint-invested firms. This tends to stem from the mature usage and experience on IT by foreign firms. Future research should consider how local firms can put

more focus on a good fit between IT physical assets and management resources.

With this little research, very strong claims cannot be made as yet about resources, e-commerce and DC firms until further research has been done.

Source: [22]

EXAMPLE 6: RESEARCH PROBLEM – ILLUSTRATING A METHOD GAP

Access to Credit by Firms in Sub-Saharan Africa: How Relevant is Gender?
Due to a paucity of data, research on the determinants of firms' financing constraints has focused on firms in developed economies (Asiedu et al. 2013). The World Bank's Enterprise Survey (WBES) of 2006 provided the first set of reliable data on firms in developing countries. This paper examines the importance of the gender of the firm's owner as a determinant of the firm's access to finance in developing countries, with a focus on sub-Saharan Africa. To the best of our knowledge, this is the first study that considers the gender of the firm's owner as a factor of firms' financing constraints across countries and regions. A few policy papers have discussed the gender gap in access to credit, but they provide only anecdotal evidence (e.g., Hallward-Driemeier, 2013). The study most closely related to our work is the paper by Aterido, Beck and Iacovone (2011). While these authors also use data from WBES, their focus is different. Specifically, they examine whether the gender of the firm's owner affects the firm's use of financial services. In this study we investigate whether female-owned firms are more financially constrained than male-owned firms.

Source: [23]

From the above examples, we can identify four key steps in formulating a research problem through a research gap. The process begins by reviewing existing literature to do the following:

1. Problem Identification - Identify the broad problem and state its importance.
2. Complement - State what is significant in what has already been written.
3. Review - Describe the gaps and select the gap you propose to fill in the existing research literature. This then creates an opportunity for you to make a contribution to the research in the area.
4. Define Research Focus - Establish your research purpose, objectives and questions.

Identifying Gaps

The primary source for research gaps is existing literature, particularly academic journal articles and industry research reports (from reputable research institutions). The gaps in journal articles are usually located in two places: the introduction and the conclusion/research limitations (see examples A and B in this section).

- **Gaps are usually presented in the introduction of the journal articles**
  These gaps focus on why it is important to read that journal article. It establishes the gaps in the previous research and points out the focus of the journal article.

EXAMPLE A: Gaps in the Introduction of a Journal Article

Impact of Mobile Phones on Micro-trading Activities

There is a preponderance of research studies documenting the business models which characterize the initial efforts of practitioners, mobile operators and banks. Academics have begun to catch up with studies seeking development solutions through mobile phones (Heeks and Jagun, 2008; Donner, 2010; Zuckerman, 2010). Some of the few studies making strides at correcting the imbalance argue that there are complexities of factors which affect the poor and hence, make it challenging for researchers to conceptualize the associated needs and impact of mobile phones with one theoretical model or theory (Aminuzzaman et al., 2003). This often contributes to the blurred distinctions between amplification and transformational effects and also between social and production (business) spheres in adoption and usage (Donner, 2007). Thus, future studies will have to draw on a more comprehensive approach to evaluate the multi-stranded impact of mobile phones on the livelihoods of adopters.

Source: [19]

- **Future Research Directions or Gaps for Future Research**
  Usually the conclusion of an academic journal article focuses on discussing the implications of the findings of the research and also point out gaps for

future research. This is important for researchers to find out the gaps pointed out by previous researchers.

EXAMPLE B: Gaps in the Conclusion of a Journal Article

Impact of Mobile Phones on Micro-trading Activities

For future research and other mobiles for development initiatives, the conceptual framework may be used to analyze mobile phones and other micro-trading activities such as taxi services in transportation, and carpenters and potters in manufacturing.

Source: [19]

Exhibit 4 illustrates an example of a research consisting of a complement, evidence from literature, and a research focus based on the gap.

Exhibit 4 Social Networking in the Public Sector in Mexico

Topic: Social Networking in the Public Sector in Mexico

The adoption of social media by the government confronts a series of barriers. Some of these barriers relate to records management, privacy and security issues, accuracy, and administration-specific requirements (Bertot *et al.*, 2012; Bryer and Zavattaro, 2011; Landsbergen, 2010 and Sherman, 2011).

As social media includes two-way communications, the risk of inserting malware into governments' websites exists (Bertot *et al.*, 2012), so the IT people should be prepared to protect government's information technology infrastructure. Governments that would like to implement social media need to verify if people in charge of updating the media will have the time to update the new communication channel; they also need to answer other questions such as what to post, how and when often they will update (Bryer and Zavattaro, 2011 and Landsbergen, 2010). The lack of resources and procedures could undermine the accuracy of the information posted on social media.

Although the use of social media in Mexican state government portals is recent, the development of relationships between government and citizens is growing fast (Sandoval-Almazán *et al.*, 2011). However, in contrast with other countries, to our knowledge, there is still no guideline for the use of social media in Mexico. The study of perceived risks, benefits, and strategies will be very helpful in the development of those guidelines.

Source: [20]

Despite where research gaps can be found, they are usually communicated as one or a combination of the following:

(1) Missing issues in literature
(2) Limited discussions in literature
(3) Conflicts in theoretical approach
(4) Missing theoretical models
(5) Conflicts/ in empirical methods (data collection and context)
(6) Mixed previous empirical results
(7) Less contextual evaluation or geographic representation
(8) Complex (limited previous results, conflicts, absence, mixed views)

Linking the Research Gaps to the Research Topic

To link the identified and selected research gap, the researcher has to define a scope for the research. For example, in an organizational study, the researcher may consider:

1. Studying one part of an organization;
2. Comparing several parts or functions of an organization;
3. Studying one organization;
4. Comparing two or more organization; and
5. Studying a sector/industry.

After the scope is defined for a research gap, the research purpose and research objectives of the research can be formulated. When the research purpose is defined, the research title can be refined or formulated to be consistent with the research purpose, see examples C and D (overleaf).

EXAMPLE C: Link between Research Purpose and Research Title

Research Topic: Financing Decisions/Capital Structure Decisions
Sub-theme: Corporate Governance
Research Title: Corporate Governance and Financing Decisions of Ghanaian Listed Firms
Level of Analysis: Micro (listed firms)
Context: Ghana
Research Purpose: It is crucial to determine how current issues in corporate governance affect the financing decisions of Ghanaian firms. This paper specifically examines the relationship between various variables of corporate governance and the capital structure decisions of firms listed on the GSE during the six-year period (1998-2003).

Example D: Link between Research Purpose and Research Title

Research Topic: Mobile Phone Adoption
Sub-theme: Micro-trading
Research Title: Mobiles and Micro-trading: Conceptualizing the Link
Level of Analysis: Micro (market traders)
Context: Ghana
Research Purpose: This study investigates the impact of mobile phones on the micro-trading activities of traders in Ghana. The study develops a conceptual model analyzing the impact of mobile phones on pre-trade, during-trade and post-trade activities.

Summary

In this chapter, we discussed how to select a research topic. Good research topics take effort to ascertain and must meet a certain kind of criteria. The good research topic must:

(1) Be original;
(2) Be of interest to both the researcher and the supervisor;
(3) Be timely and relevant;
(4) It must make a contribution to existing knowledge or respond to a research gap;
(5) Be specific and distinct, not too broad;
(6) Incorporate the main purpose of the research;
(7) Be clever, captivating and unforgettable; and
(8) The research questions that flow from it must be possible to address through a research design.

We also explained the concept of research gaps and their relevance in research. Research gaps are the discrepancies in existing research literature which need to be addressed. A complex gap consisting of an issue and context can help undergraduate and graduate students establish a good basis for their research.

In the next chapter we will discuss literature review.

Richard Boateng

Chapter Discussions

Mobiles and Micro-Trading: Conceptualizing the Link

There has been a tremendous growth in mobile phone ownership and use globally. Statistics from the International Telecommunication Union tend to suggest that mobile phone subscribers currently constitute 60 percent of the world population (ITU, 2008a). The rapid diffusion of this relatively low-cost technology has spurred a development agenda questioning how mobile phones can be harnessed more effectively for socio-economic development in developing economies and other resource-poor contexts.

Initial efforts in finding answers to these questions can be analyzed from two perspectives: the practitioner and academic research perspectives. The initiatives of mobile network operators, banks, entrepreneurs, governments and development agencies characterize efforts from the practitioner perspective. These efforts tend to focus on the design and adoption of mobile applications for micro-finance activities or to enhance access to financial services (Donner, 2008; CGAP, 2008). Efforts addressing the impact of mobiles on development concerns and needs – combating poverty and stimulating economic growth – are quite few. This imbalance is also reflected on the academic research front (Duncombe and Boateng, 2009). There is a preponderance of research studies documenting the business models which characterize the initial efforts of practitioners, mobile operators and banks. Academics have begun to catch up with studies seeking development solutions through mobile phones (Heeks and Jagun, 2008; Donner, 2010; Zuckerman, 2010). Some of the few studies making strides at correcting the imbalance argue that there are complexities of factors which affect the poor and hence, make it challenging for researchers to conceptualize the associated needs and impact of mobile phones with one theoretical model or theory. (Aminuzzaman et al., 2003). This often contributes to the blurred distinctions between amplification and transformational effects, and also between social and production (business) spheres in adoption and usage (Donner, 2007).

Thus, future studies will have to draw on a more comprehensive approach to evaluate the multi-stranded impact of mobile phones on the livelihoods of adopters.

Source: [19]

QUESTION 1

Using the above research problem explain the concept of a research gap and discuss two research gaps from the above research problem.

CHAPTER 3

Reviewing The Past to Determine The Future

Objectives

The literature review usually provides a detailed analysis of the research topic from the perspective of existing literature, identifies gaps and, further, critiques and proposes perspectives or ways of addressing the research problem. This chapter provides direction to researchers on how to conduct literature reviews.

Literature Review Defined

THERE ARE A number of definitions for literature review. The different definitions tend to emphasize a number of different requirements for the content of a literature review. However, in this book, I will adopt a definition which attempts to bring together all the different requirements in one brief sentence. A literature review (LR) can be defined as:

> "A synthesis of available resources and materials with a strong rela-
> tion to the topic in question, accompanied by a description and a criti-
> cal evaluation and comparative analysis of each work" [24].

This definition has a number of components, hence; let us try to analyze the defini-tion. First, LR is a **synthesis**. According to the Merriam-Webster dictionary, the word 'synthesis', refers to "the composition or combination of parts or elements so as to form a whole; or the combining of often diverse conceptions into a coherent whole" [25]. This means literature review requires the researcher to bring two or more things to together to form a whole. LR cannot consist of just one thing; at least there should be two.

Second, what is this thing, or what is the researcher expected to combine. The above definition states that the researcher is required to bring together '**available re-sources and materials**'. Availability as used here refers to accessibility. Thus, the re-searcher is required to bring together accessible literature resources and materials. It is important for the resources and materials to have a degree of accessibility so that, they can be verified, checked or referred to by other researchers. This can be accomplished through the provision of references to the materials and resources used. References provide the source of the materials and resources. The researcher is expected to use more than one resource, and preferably, diverse resources so that the LR reflects a diversity of perspectives which are critically and comparatively reflected. Further, to a large extent, it is good practice for the available materials and resources to be pub-lished works.

Third, the materials and resources selected are required to have a '**strong rela-tion to the topic in question**'. Thus, LR needs a focus. The synthesis should cover literature relevant to the topic in question or topic which the researcher is researching on. For example, a researcher researching on the impact of mining companies in rural communities will need to synthesize literature on the mining or extractive industry. This said, literature on space exploration is not relevant to such a research study.

Fourth, LR is not just a list of relevant resources and materials. The relevant resources and materials have to be **described** or summarized, **critically** and **comparatively** evaluated. It is important to note that a LR is not a comprehensive list of books and articles pertaining to a particular discipline/topic nor is it an annotated bibliography. The definition states that, the list of available resources and materials should be **accompanied by a description and a critical evaluation and comparative analysis of each work**. Describing the literature requires the researcher to summarize what other researchers have found. Some researchers provide a chronological list of what has been found and when it was found. However, this is not good enough for an analytical LR. The analytical review requires the researcher to synthesize and pass judgment on the merits of the previous research on the topic in question, reveal gaps and limitations, recognize future research directions or opportunities, and justify choices made by the researcher concerning how the researcher intends to address the topic in question. These differences in descriptive and analytical (critical and comparative) review are illustrated in Exhibit 5. Though both reviews are chronological, the analytical review synthesizes and critically reviews existing literature to identify comparable and contrasting perspectives on the topic under question. The author begins with a summary argument on the trends on literature on unemployment in Africa. This was followed up by a chronological description of evidence (references) with comparative illustrations. The author concludes with an argument which abstracts the essence of the evidences presented in the review. Hence, chronological description and comparative illustrations lead to the concluding argument that, "<u>unemployment in Africa may be viewed from a multi-facet perspective. It cannot be reduced to one single factor</u>".

EXHIBIT 5 DESCRIPTIVE AND ANALYTICAL REVIEWS

Descriptive Review

A study by Uche (2000) on unemployment in the banking industry in Nigeria highlighted that inflation affected the turnover of banks which had also had an effect on salary payments. Over 2000 bank employees lost their jobs by the end of 1999. Thakur (2005) discussed that lack of capital for start-up initiatives and high interest rates on loans stalled entrepreneurial ventures and contributed to unemployment or the lack of job opportunities. In a recent study on unemployment in Egypt, Salia (2011) found political instability, poor governance and lack of foreign direct investment to be the critical factors influencing unemployment.

Analytical Review

Literature demonstrates that the key factors which contribute to unemployment in Africa have tended to change over time. In the late 1990s researchers argued that inflation and low wages contributed to unemployment (Uche, 2000; Benson, 2003). A study by Uche (2000) on unemployment in the banking industry in Nigeria highlighted that inflation affected the turnover of banks which had also had an effect in salary payments. Over 2000 bank employees lost their jobs by the end of 1999.

On the other hand, by 2004, researchers discussed that lack of capital for start-up initiatives and high interest rates on loans stalled entrepreneurial ventures and contributed to unemployment or the lack of job opportunities (Thakur, 2005). A comparative study (Kinson, 2006) on the SME industry in Ghana and Uganda shared similar findings on the effects of start-up capital and interest loans on entrepreneurship and unemployment. In a recent study on unemployment in Egypt, Salia (2011) found political instability, poor governance and lack of foreign direct investment to be the critical factors influencing unemployment. Other studies in Cote d'Ivoire and Sierra Leone attest to these findings (Johnson, 2009; Pern, 2010).

In effect, unemployment in Africa may be viewed from a multi-facet perspective. It cannot be reduced to one single factor.

From the above explanation of the definition of LR, it can be identified that LR may require researchers to explain the concepts and issues in research; discuss the main relevant arguments concerning the issues; draw on existing and current research on the issues and discuss their findings and how they help us better understand the issues; review research in specific/diverse geographic contexts to highlight what has been done; and explain how previous research was conducted: which frameworks and methods were used.

Why Do Literature Review

Researchers often argue that, they have enough knowledge about their area of research. However, they find themselves short of ideas as soon as they begin to write on their topics. LR is therefore relevant to researchers for a number of reasons, namely

- To justify your research.
- To show awareness of the present state of knowledge of a particular field.
- To provide a foundation for the research.

In justifying the reason for one's research area or topic, the process of literature review helps to demonstrate the necessity for a particular research. This helps to answer the questions "And so what or what is new in your research?" During the stage of literature review, gaps in extant research are revealed which merit a closer investigation. Hence, justifying the reason for your research; since by filling these gaps, the study will add to the body of knowledge in the field. However, filling the gaps is not a good justification but rather the reasons for filling the gaps, and it is through literature review that these justifications can be revealed and appropriately illustrated [26]. Through the literature review process of extensive reading and analysis you can prove that your work hasn't been previously done and it is indeed original [24].

Second, another reason for reviewing literature is to demonstrate your awareness of the present state of knowledge. In demonstrating awareness, you look at the current trends in the field of study and the authors who are spearheading those studies and their recommendations for future research. Thus in reviewing literature I don't only examine who has written what, but the main empirical research, theoretical positions, controversies, and breakthroughs, as well as links with other related areas of knowledge [27]. In addition, the process helps the individual to gain information seeking and critical appraisal skills and knowledge through rigorous scanning of literature and the ability to synthesize vital information from materials and resources [28].

Third, LR provides a foundation for the research by enabling the researcher to identify and discuss relevant research questions to be asked, and the theories and methods to be used. For example, through a literature review, a study about technology adoption could reveal prominent theories like the Technology Acceptance Model as an important construct which in turn can become the central foundation of the study.

In effect, a thorough literature review process helps the researcher to narrow the research focus, pose questions that might not have previously occurred to the researcher, prove originality and significance, and build a knowledge base for future research. The diversity of literature sources also tends to demonstrate that the researcher has read extensively on the topic in question.

Steps in Literature Review

Some researchers find the literature review process to be a herculean task to accomplish. In this section, I will provide some guidelines for the LR process. The stages are iterative, as flexibility is required to make the process successful. The steps are to:

1. Decide on a topic
2. Identify, Locate literature
   - Categorize Literature
3. Ensure Relevance
4. Record and Retrieve
5. Review and Summarize
6. Write and revise a topic

SELECT AND REFINE A TOPIC

Every research must begin with a topic or theme so that the researcher knows the direction the research should follow. Without a topic, theme or area of interest, it becomes difficult to direct efforts towards a particular area and gather literature in its regard. However, if a theme, topic or area of study is identified then, the process of literature gathering can commence.

IDENTIFY AND LOCATE LITERATURE

Define your keywords
Once the topic, theme or field of study is identified and refined, the process of identifying and locating literature begins. Develop some keywords if necessary - words or short phrases that describe the topic of your search. For example, you want to write a research on the sources of financing of small and medium enterprises in the manufacturing sector. Your starter keywords might be – Manufacturing SMEs, SME financing, and manufacturing financing.

You can think of more keyword terms in three ways:

a) Broader - i.e. "SME challenges" is broader than "SME financing"
b) Narrower - i.e. "SME financing" and "small business financing" are narrower than "financing";
c) Related - i.e. "entrepreneurs" or "small business" are related to "small and medium enterprises"

Define the boundaries, constraints or limitations of your search

TIME
You can set your time boundary in two ways:

- Forwards - By answering, "How much time is it worth spending on this search?"
- Backwards - By answering, "How much time is available to complete this task?"

TYPE OF MATERIAL
When you are doing your information search, you have to decide whether you are looking for primary or secondary sources[2]. The basic difference is that

- *Primary* sources are usually a direct record of observations or findings; written by the person who observes - For example, letters, interviews, census data, reports on visits.
- *Secondary* sources are normally written after the event. Most reports of research are secondary sources - journal articles, dissertations of original fieldwork.
- Textbooks and dissertations which summarize from various research reports should be referred to as *tertiary* sources.

---

2 Credit to University of Manchester Development Informatics Cluster's Dissertation Guidelines

Examples of these sources are subsequently outlined as follows: Sources of Information

a) **Search engines**: www.google.com; www.scholar.google.com
b) **Online databases:**
Examples of electronic databases include:

Subscription Databases

1. EBSCOhost: www.search.epnet.com
2. Emerald: www.emeralinsight.com
3. JSTOR: www.jstor.org
4. Palgrave Macmillan Journals: www.palgrave-journals.com
5. Sage Journals Online: www.online.sagepub.com
6. ScienceDirect – www.sciencedirect.com
7. Wiley – www.onlinelibrary.wiley.com

   Students can contact the university libraries for a more comprehensive list. For example in University of Ghana, Electronic Databases can be accessed through:
   - http://library.ug.edu.gh/screens/balme/oncampus.html or
   - http://tinyurl.com/ugjournals

Free/Limited Access Databases

8. African Journals Online (AJOL): www.ajolonline.com
9. Directory of Open Access Journals (DOAJ): http://doaj.org/
10. Google Scholar (Multidisciplinary): www.scholar.google.com
11. Social Science Research Network: www.ssrn.com/
12. Topics in Development: www.worldbank.org/en/topic

Online Statistical Sources

There are a number of online statistical sources; e.g. accessible via:
- Global: World Bank Databases: http://data.worldbank.org/
- In Ghana: http://www.statsghana.gov.gh/

c) Specialist Websites
- Information Systems World - ISWorld: http://www.isworld.org/
- Academy of Marketing - http://www.academyofmarketing.org/
- Institute of Electrical and Electronics Engineers - IEEE Xplore Digital Library - www.ieeexplore.ieee.org
- Association for Computing Machinery Digital Library - www.dl.acm.org
- Research students can ask their supervisors or other senior researchers for information on specialist websites for their respective disciplines.

d) Online search access for **key newspapers and other news sources**, including Wall Street Journal, The Economist, Financial Times and news sources:

e) Source guides/bibliographies/'Review of...': give guidance on literature sources in a particular topic area.

f) Citation index: allows you to search forwards in time from a classic text/article by showing other sources (general journal articles) that cite the classic in their bibliographies. You can access the most likely one to be of value – Social Sciences Citation Index – at: http://portal.isiknowledge.com

g) Lecture handouts

h) Your supervisor

Boundaries such as time, year of publication, type of material, source et cetera may change with time if the initial boundaries fail to produce enough information. For search engines (including databases) you will be well served if you learn how to do more advanced searches: using terms AND, OR and NOT.

Secondary Sources of Information

Relevant literature for a research paper, dissertation, long essay or thesis may be obtained from:

- **Scholarly journals and conference papers**: these resources are arguably the most relevant resource for academic work. They provide peer-reviewed articles which critically review research topics from a contemporary perspective. Conference papers provide emerging perspectives of research topics, which are yet to be published in journals[3].
- **Books**: these resources are good for understanding concepts, theories and conceptual frameworks.
- **Dissertations**: These resources are relevant to obtain an explanation of concepts and act as examples of research work done by a student. Sometimes students tend to plagiarize from existing research. This is not advisable. The resources should be used to learn how to structure their essays or theses or not for plagiarism.
- **Government documents, Periodicals, Policy reports and Industry Reports**: These resources provide statistics and background information relevant for writing the research background and describing the context of a study or a research problem.
- **Newspaper/periodical articles:** Uncertain accuracy; easy to access; useful for chronology of events; useful for pointers to further investigation.

Primary Sources of Information

- **Statistical/survey information** (e.g. census data). Useful for estimation; useful to check accuracy; cannot substitute for your own original survey work. May be available via the Web or on CD-ROM.
- **Information on individual 'units of enquiry'** (e.g. interviews, employment records, health records). Rich in information; very hard to access unless/even

---

3 Not all journals are reliable. Kindly refer to the appendix for information on refereed journals.

if you are an employee in the same organization or have a contact in that organization.

- **Case records** (e.g. educational records, project summaries). Rich in information, but may not be representative of whole population; information recorded may not match that required by research; subjective opinion contained; hard to access.
- **Personal documents** (e.g. diaries, letters, and essays). Rich in information; provide individual insight; can be biased and subjective.
- **Formal records** (e.g. minutes of meetings, committee reports). Represents summary of viewpoints; may miss out a real, political, subjective picture; hard to access outside the organization concerned.

Places to Access Data

- The Web
- Libraries – University Library
- Organizations – the one being studied; other (university/other research centers, government, company, trade associations, chambers of commerce, professional associations, NGOs, trade unions).

Publication Date
This decision may depend on how up-to-date you need the information to be. For example, you may choose to only search material published within the last five years. I do recommend that if you are reviewing literature to establish research gaps and justify your research purpose, your literature search should primarily seek to be contemporary or recent. Thus, papers published within the last five years, maximum seven years, should be your primary focus. Gaps echoed in literature published more than seven years ago are likely to have been addressed or reiterated in more recent literature.

Language
The default languages for communication for the researcher and for the online database are likely to determine the language to be used for the search. That said, there could be

exceptions, especially with primary data. In such cases, the researcher may need to get the information translated in order to use it in the research study. Not all online databases support multiple languages. I personally only know about EBSCOhost; it is multilingual.

Geographical Focus

I do recommend that students develop a global perspective of the topic in question, before narrowing down to a specific geographic region, or country. For example, you can search for items on Ghana in order to establish what has been done in Ghana concerning your topic. However, you cannot only build your research purpose on those items; it is necessary to consider findings and recommendations from other geographical contexts. If you do so, you may find out that your research gap has been addressed in literature on your research topic but conducted in other countries. Hence, the originality of your research work has just been thrown out through the window.

Doing the Search

Exhibit 6 Searching for Journal Articles

1. Go to the journal database
2. Use the search box
   - Basic Search
   - Advanced Search
3. Type in your research topic
4. Review results
   - Check Relevance
   - Refine search parameters
5. Record and Retrieve
6. Review and Summarize

Richard Boateng

Finding literature is now made easier through the advancement of technology. The best part is that, most of these sources are available in electronic format which facilitate easy and quicker access to these materials. In searching for literature, keywords, themes, and phrases pertaining to the topic under study should be used to narrow the search. The literature can be obtained through electronic/online databases. Online databases offer both basic and advanced search options. Advanced search is preferable, since it offers the opportunity to narrow search parameters by journal, abstract, article title and year (see steps provided in Exhibit 6 and 7).

Exhibit 7 Advanced Search for Journal Articles in Emerald Insight Database

Advanced search

Search in   All   **Journals**   Books   Case Studies

Search for

poverty and unemployment

in   All fields ▼

> All fields
> All except full text
> Abstract
> Journal title
> Special issue title
> Article title
> Author
> ISSN
> Volume
> Issue
> Page
> Keywords

ny ○ Phrase

ny ○ Phrase

Match: ● All ○ Any ○ Phrase

Limit the search to:

Items published between:

All ▼   and   All ▼

Article type:

All Types ▼

Include in results:

EarlyCite Articles ✔ Emerald Backfiles ✔

Ensure Relevance - Prioritizing information sources

Although finding the material has been facilitated by technology, irrelevant materials are also available; hence, the task of filtering through available materials, to ensure that only relevant materials are used in the literature review. If you feel that there are too many sources of information for you to cover them effectively in the time available, then you must prioritize them. Read the titles and abstracts and prioritize the literature according to the relevance they have to the topic in question - high, medium or low priority. High priority refers to literature which has a direct significance or relationship to the topic. For example, a research on SME financing in the manufacturing sector may consider every publication on SME financing as either high or medium priority. The publications which focus on the manufacturing sector could be considered high priority or those which focus on SME financing in Ghana may also be considered high priority. However, a publication which broadly discusses the challenges of SMEs and outlines financing as one of the challenges may be considered either as medium priority (especially if the study was conducted in Ghana) or low priority. Most often, low priority publications only tend to provide a definition of a concept, a statistic or a statement which can be used to support arguments from medium and high priority publications. The judgment depends on the researcher, purpose of the review, and may also differ depending on the stage/step of the research process the researcher has reached. For example in the extract below, Salia (2011) may be considered as a high priority publication and Johnson (2009) and Pern (2010) may be considered either medium or low priority publications.

> In a recent study on unemployment in Egypt, Salia (2011) found political instability, poor governance and lack of foreign direct investment to be the critical factors influencing unemployment. Other studies in Cote d'Ivoire and Sierra Leone attest to these findings (Johnson, 2009; Pern, 2010).

The researcher is also advised to remember to stick to the parameters/boundaries that were set before the search - e.g. just focus on the most recent material. Hence, there is need to develop the habit of screening the literature for relevance before downloading it or printing it out. This way the researcher will not become overwhelmed with all of the reading that they have to do.

RECORD AND RETRIEVE

Literature which is identified as relevant to the study is downloaded and saved for future reference. Since most materials required in the literature review process are now in electronic format it becomes easy to download and save them. This process is essential to the literature review process, as relevant materials to the study need to be retained for future use. If you don't save relevant materials, it will become difficult to get them and use if the need arises. Moreover, the downloaded materials should be classified and saved with relevant names for easy identification (classification and categorization are discussed later in the chapter).

REVIEW AND SUMMARIZE

Review and summarization involves the process of reading and eliciting ideas relevant to your research from available material. But these ideas must be summarized without losing the focal point of the material.

Summarizing an Article to a Page

In summarizing an article to a page for the purpose of a literature review, the following information should be considered.

1. Article Reference:
   a) ALWAYS remember to record the bibliographic details of all references or other information sources (even if they are not useful) - perhaps on card:
      i. Journal Article: Author Last name, Other initials (year of publication) Title of the journal article, Name of the Journal, Volume/Number, page range
      ii. Book: author, title, edition, publisher, place of publication, date
      iii. Report: author, title, report number, issuing organization, place of publication, date
      iv. Interview/Conversation: name, job title, date, organization, place
      v. Online document: author, page/document title, site-owning organization, organization's physical city location, date of writing/publication, URL, date of access
2. Research Problem/Research Question(s)
3. Research Frameworks Used
4. Research Methods
5. Results/Findings and Discussions
6. Conclusions
7. Gaps for Future Research

Exhibit 8 is an example of a one-page summary of an article.

Exhibit 8 One Page Summary of an Article

Article Title: Aminuzzaman, Baldersheim, & Jamil (2003) Talking back: Empowerment and mobile phones in rural Bangladesh: A study of the village pay phone of the Grameen Bank, *Contemporary South Asia* 12:3.

Research Questions

The study assesses the efficacy of the Village Phone (VP) scheme in ameliorating the 'information poverty' of the villages that have obtained access to mobile phones in Bangladesh. **Identification of processes that influence the success of the village phone operations.**

Concepts/Theories/frameworks employed

Concept: **'Information Poverty'** - a situation in which an inadequate telecommunications infrastructure leads to limitations on the choices available to individuals because high costs of communications makes it too costly to seek out information about alternative courses of action. VP is expected to be a **'ripple-effect technology'** - one with a multi-stranded impact rather than one that creates pockets of modernization in a traditional society. In ripple-effect technologies, impacts spread cumulatively across many aspects of the life of individuals and communities, starting a transformative process of development.

Theory: theory of **asymmetrical information and cultural perspectives on collective action**, plus literature review on previous experiences with technology-driven development projects.

    Model: Analytical Model of Village Phone Intervention (demand-and-supply model)

Methods used

Bangladesh - survey of 350 VP owners/operators and users (in our project, 20 different locations were chosen for closer study, 158 users were surveyed, and so were 85 operators, 55 key informants, 75 distant beneficiaries and 50 respondents from control areas).

Data collected: a) Profile of VP stakeholders; (b) Call patterns; (c) Impact of the VP

Issues addressed
Identification of processes that influence the success of the village phone operations.

- What are the factors that make for success or failure in an intervention of the type that the VP represents; that is, a technology-driven development initiative?

Findings/Discussions
The calls, therefore, are probably driven mostly by professional and economic motives. Social motives top the list of purposes of the calls made. Of these, it is calls to family members and relatives that dominate. Followed by business.

Research Gaps
Blurred distinctions between social and business use of mobile phones. Impact is multi-stranded and needs a multi-facet research approach in terms of theory and methods.

Making Good Reference Notes
For an information search, you could also note down from your reading other references, individuals or organizations which seem useful. You may also notice certain journal names recurring - then go to the journal and look through recent issues. Some researchers recommend the use of 'spider diagrams' or mind maps to develop notes concerning the topic in question [29]. In this case, the objective is to summarize a lot of information on one page in a visual and memorable way. Put the main topic in the middle and add key words on the "arms" of the diagram – the key thing is to keep it brief. The key advantages of mind maps are that they show the main points at a glance, and help keep points grouped together; thereby structuring your thoughts and also clearly showing where there are gaps which need more research.

Exhibit 9 Spider Diagram or Mind map

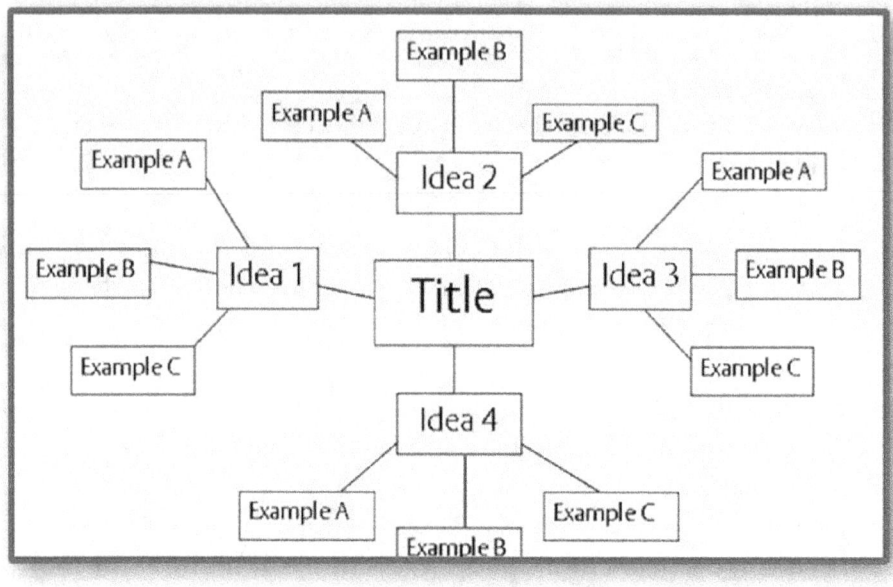

Source: [29]

Write

The final stage of the literature review process is writing. Most students find themselves copying and repeating what they find in literature, therefore efforts should be made to avoid these mistakes. Use the results of your analysis and critique of the literature to develop the organization of your review.

The next section of this chapter will provide guidelines on how to categorize literature, analyze and write analytically.

Categorizing Literature

Now you have found a lot of relevant literature so what next? Categorization is required to organize the materials. This can be done in a number of ways, depending on the purpose of the review. The key categories are summarized in Exhibit 10.

EXHIBIT 10 CATEGORIZING LITERATURE

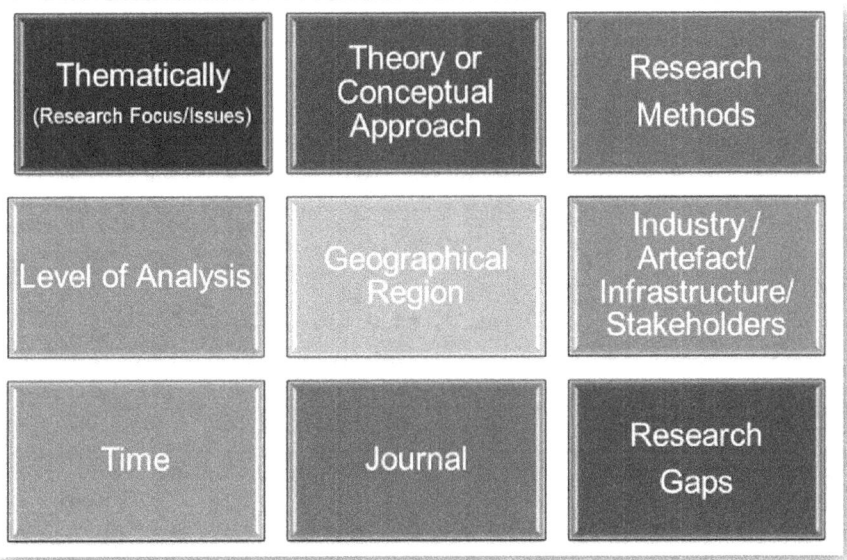

THEMATICALLY

The downloaded literature is categorized according to sub-themes concerning the research topic. The themes may be derived from previous literature reviews, keywords used in the downloaded literature, or a particular model used to explain the topic. In my publications on the review of e-commerce in developing countries (DCs), I categorized by topic into three major themes with sub-themes (See Exhibits 11 and 12) [30] [31].

EXHIBIT 11 DISTRIBUTION OF E-COMMERCE IN DCs RESEARCH ARTICLES BY THEMES

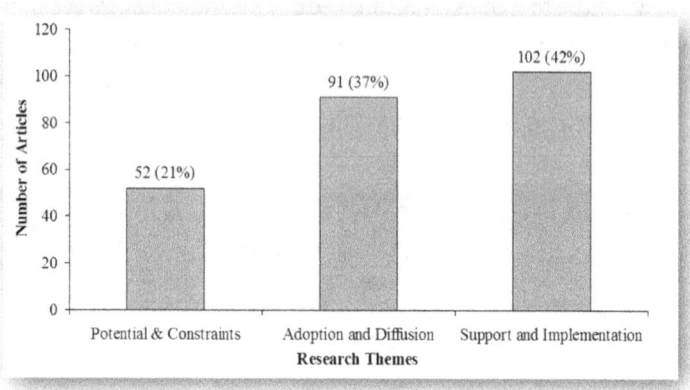

Source: [22]

EXHIBIT 12 DISTRIBUTION OF E-COMMERCE IN DCs RESEARCH ARTICLES BY SUB-THEMES

Research Focus		Number of Articles
Potential & Constraints		41 (23%)
	- Opportunities	19 (10%)
	- Assessment	17 (9%)
	- Development	5 (3%)
Adoption and Diffusion		66 (36%)
	- Technology	19 (10%)
	- Managerial	6 (3%)
	- Organizational	2 (1%)
	- Cultural	6 (3%)
	- Environmental	9 (5%)
	- E-readiness	3 (2%)
	- Interaction	21 (12%)
Support and Implementation		69 (38%)
	- Consumer Behaviour	4 (2%)
	- Design and Development	4 (2%)
	- Public Policy – Legal	3 (2%)
	- Public Policy – Security & Trust	4 (2%)
	- Public Policy – Taxation	2 (1%)
	- Service Evaluation	6 (3%)
	- Organizational and Industrial Strategy	25 (14%)
	- National and Regional Strategy	21 (12%)
Education		4 (2%)
Knowledge Management		1 (1%)
Total		181 (100%)

Source: [31]

The distribution by sub-themes (Exhibit 12) tends to offer more insight on the research work done within each theme; providing insight into the seemingly dominant and less-dominant research themes.

For example, from the above, the bulk of articles on support and implementation have focused on strategy issues, with 25 articles (14%) on organizational and industrial strategy, and 21 articles (12%) on national and regional strategy. The less represented articles are on security and trust issues, 4 articles (2%); legal issues, 3 articles (2%); and taxation issues, 2 articles (1%), under public policy. The focus of future research on public policy issues can be on investigating the low adoption of less dominating e-commerce applications, including electronic payment systems and Internet-based auctions in DCs.

On the other hand, in pure-numbers a less-researched theme does not necessarily mean it is most attractive for research contribution. Sometimes a less-researched theme may reflect the lack of research focus which may stem from the immaturity of the topic with regard to the context or geographic region being studied. For example, the above review in Exhibit 12 consisted of articles published from 1993 to 2005. Arguably, e-commerce in most developing countries is a post-2000 phenomenon, hence, by 2005; most developing countries were still struggling with issues on adoption. Thus, public policy issues such as taxation, legal, and security, were still in its infancy in both practice and policy. Further, since academics are usually catching up to what is happening in practice, research on these themes is likely to be far-fetched.

Consequently, it is important that research themes are cross-tabulated with other categories such as time, level-of-analysis, theory or geographic region or focus in-order to better understand where and why the gaps exist.

TIME

The downloaded literature can be categorized according to the year of publication. For example, my categorization of e-commerce in developing countries literature by year of publication demonstrated that scanty e-commerce research was carried out in DCs before 1999 and there has been an appreciable increase since 2000 (Exhibit 13) [30].

Exhibit 13 Distribution of E-commerce in DCs Research Articles by Year

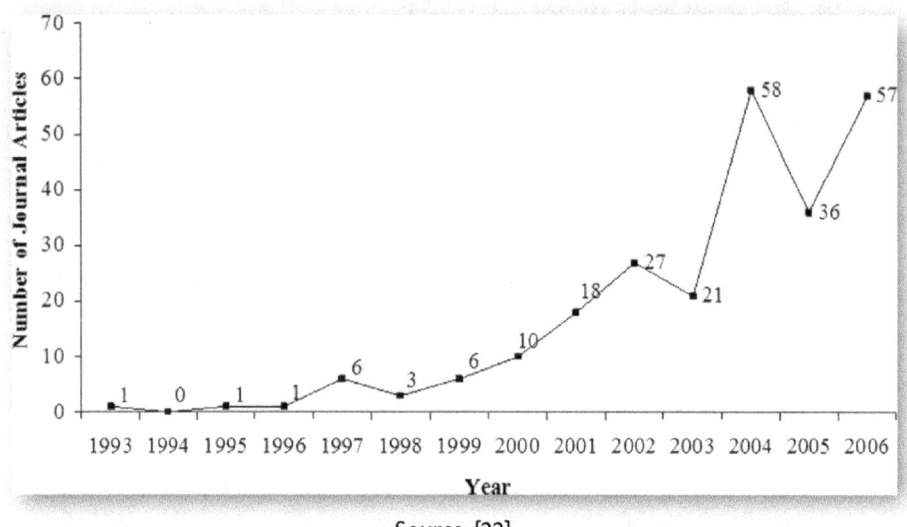

Source: [22]

Theories and Conceptual Approaches

A theory is a "coherent set of general propositions used as principles of explanation, understanding and/or prediction of the apparent relationships of certain observed phenomena" [32]. Conceptual frameworks or approaches are analytical schemes which simplify reality to make it easier to discuss, analyze or research. They simplify reality by selecting certain phenomena/variables and suggesting certain relationships between them [33]. Theories and conceptual frameworks can be categorized according to their purpose of application, type (constituents/origin) or degree of theorization.

Purpose of Application: The purpose refers to what or how the theory is applied. For example, a technology adoption theory or framework will seek to explain technology adoption; whilst a strategy theory will seek to explain organizational strategy (see Exhibit 14).

Exhibit 14 Distribution of E-commerce in DCs Research Articles by Theory

Theoretical/Conceptual Frameworks	Number of Articles
Group One – Assessment of Opportunities and Evaluation of Benefits	
Transaction Cost Theory (reviewed in Pare, 2003)	4
Economic Theory on Online Shopping (reviewed Mahmood *et al.*, 2004)	1
Group Two – Adoption, Diffusion, Consumer Behavior, and Service Evaluation	
Technology Acceptance Model (TAM) (Davis, 1985)	12
Technology-Organization-Environment (Tornatzky and Fleischer, 1990)	9
Diffusion of Innovation (Rogers, 1983)	7
Hofstede's Cultural Framework (Hofstede, 1980)	7
Theory of Planned Behavior (Ajzen, 1991)	5
Group Three – Strategy	
Resource Based Theory (Barney, 1991; Teece *et al.*, 1997)	3
DeLone and Mclean's IS Success Model (Molla and Licker, 2001)	1
Group Four – Public Policy, Infrastructure and Others	21
Frameworks include Three Layers of E-commerce Network (Singh and Gilchrist, 2002); Privacy-Trust-Behavioral Intentions Model (Liu *et al.*, 2004);	

In close examination, Group Two consists of theoretical frameworks used in studying issues relating to adoption, diffusion, consumer behavior, and service evaluation. Three major theories, diffusion of innovation, theory of planned behavior, and theory of reasoned action tend to be the underpinning theories of quite a number of adoption and diffusion theoretical frameworks research models including the technology acceptance model (12 articles). As a result e-commerce research on adoption and diffusion have a fundamental theoretical understanding which facilitates the easier formulation of research models, their replication in research in different developing countries and makes the knowledge contributed more theoretically and practically grounded.

Type (constituents/origin): The type refers to the origin of the theory or conceptual framework or what the constructs or constituents of the theory tend to depict. For example, some theories or conceptual approaches may be considered to be underpinned by social factors, technical factors or socio-technical factors. Thus, both the social and technical parameters can be used as categories along a spectrum. These categories may include: a) social systems – concerned with underlying socio-economic and cultural factors; b) socio-technical systems – concerned with understanding the interrelationships between social systems and technologies; c) technical systems associated with understanding the design, development and adaptability of the technologies themselves.

For example, in my co-authored review of mobile finance (m-finance) in developing countries literature, the literature was mapped by conceptual approaches (type) and methodological approach. This is also an example of cross-tabulating or mapping the categories to gain a better understanding (Exhibit 15) [34].

Exhibit 15 Mapping M-finance Research by Conceptual and Methodological Approaches

	Approaches inspired by social theories	Approaches inspired by socio-technical theories (inc business models)	Approaches inspired by technical theories	No defined theoretical approach evident
Quantitative	37	11, 34, 33, 32		
Mixed methods	1, 4, 18	7		5, 21
Qualitative	2, 17, 28	35, 43	38	3, 36
Descriptive: No defined methodological approach evident	6, 25, 26	8, 9, 16, 29, 42	13, 23, 31	10, 12, 14, 15, 19, 20, 22, 24, 27, 30, 39, 40, 41

Bold: Studies analysing primary data (17 articles)

In close examination, the literature is numbered and the numbers are used in the mapping. The broad initial categorization from social to technical and no theory provided a valuable initial understanding for representing the diversity of conceptual approaches identified, indicating a spread across all three categories. It confirmed that 17 of the studies made no recourse to theory (the majority) or definable conceptual ideas and identified only four studies inspired by technical concepts.

Degree of Theorization: The conceptual approaches can also be differentiated according to a hierarchy moving from a shallower conceptualization to deeper theoretically-based approaches – as follows [35]:

- *Theoretically-based approaches*: approaches which make clear use of an identifiable theory that can be applied or tested.
- *Framework-based approaches*: approaches that make use of a framework for analysis that is derived from a body of theoretical work.
- *Model-based approaches*: models that are applied, but without reference to a deeper body of knowledge.
- *Concept-based approaches*: approaches that make use of a defined concept such as 'information poverty', but which is not theoretically grounded.
- *Category based approaches*: approaches that make use of a prescribed set of factors to carry out an analysis.

For example, in my co-authored review of mobile finance (m-finance) in developing countries literature, the literature was also mapped based on the degree of theorization in order to have a better understanding of how the conceptual approaches have been used in previous research (Exhibit 16) [34].

EXHIBIT 16 MAPPING CONCEPTUAL APPROACHES TO M-FINANCE RESEARCH IN DCS

Research Issue	Conceptual Approaches Identified	Classification	Antecedents cited
Adoption	Diffusion of innovations theory: the decomposed theory of planned behavior	Framework	Rogers (1983); Taylor & Todd (1995)
	Technology acceptance model; subjective security; task-technology-fit	Framework	Davis et al (1989)
Impact	Additive-transformational m-payment model	Model	None
	Ripple-effect technology	Concept	None

In close examination, much more prevalent is shallow theory which takes the form of framework or model based approaches (17 out of 26 articles). These include the technology acceptance model (TAM). The TAM has been used particularly to provide conceptual underpinning for studies on m-finance adoption such as Brown *et al.* (2003) who define and test a range of factors (e.g. relative advantage, compatibility, complexity and trialability) in relation to a study of early adopters undertaken in South Africa. Other models have been tailored specifically for m-finance research in a development context. Most prominent is the additive-transformational m-payment model which has been used as a practitioner tool, as well as an underlying concept in research on m-payment systems, focusing on the need for remittances of small value, application design, and classifying impact.

Methodology: Research methodology categorization is done on the basis of qualitative, quantitative or mixed methodology (see Exhibit 15 on the previous pages).

Closely examining Exhibit 15, the sample of 43 articles contains 17 peer reviewed research studies and 26 non-peer reviewed. 24 studies (six of which were peer reviewed) were purely descriptive accounts in which no approach to methodology was discernable. Thus, the number of studies employing a rigorous approach to methodology for the collection and analysis of primary data are a small proportion of the reviewed articles as a whole.

Research methodology categorization can also be done according to research methods. For example, in my review of e-commerce in DCs literature, I categorized the literature according to the research methods used (Exhibit 17) [31].

EXHIBIT 17 DISTRIBUTIONS OF E-COMMERCE IN DCs ARTICLES BY
RESEARCH METHODS

Research Methods	Number of Articles
Survey	62 (34%)
Case Study	44 (24%)
Content Analysis	1 (1%)
Archival Data Analysis	1 (1%)
Attribute Analysis	1 (1%)
Simulation/Experimental Study	4 (2%)
Mixed Methods	10 (6%)
Other (Not directly related to the above)	57 (31%)
Total	181 (100%)

Source: [31]

In close examination, the most commonly employed research methods in
e-commerce research in DCs include: survey, 62 articles (34%) and case study,
44 articles (24%). Mixed methods are also fairly represented forming 6% of
articles (10 articles). Less represented research methods include content analysis, 1 article (1%); archival or historical data analysis, 1 article (1%); and attribute analysis, 2 articles (1%). Simulation or experimental studies employed in
design and development of e-commerce technologies, education and training and in studying consumer behavior covers 2% of the articles (4 articles).

LEVEL OF ANALYSIS

A further issue of classification concerns the level of analysis at which the research is
carried out, and the extent to which the research identifies interrelationships between
levels of analysis. This can range from:

- The **micro level** – where the focus of research would be the organizational/
  firm-level (or sometimes individual-level depending on the research topic).

- The **meso level** – where the focus would be on the industry or network of firms beyond one single firm.
- The **macro level** – where the focus would be on the national-level, examining the role of institutions that deliver infrastructure, determine policy, and set rules and regulations.
- The **meta level** – where the focus is beyond one country to a regional or sometimes global or cross-country level of analysis.

Categorization by level of analysis tends to be more informative and analytical when it is mapped with research theme or geographical focus or context. In my m-finance review, research theme was mapped with level of analysis to develop a better understanding of the research themes (Exhibit 18):

EXHIBIT 18 MAPPING OF M-FINANCE RESEARCH THEMES BY LEVEL OF ANALYSIS

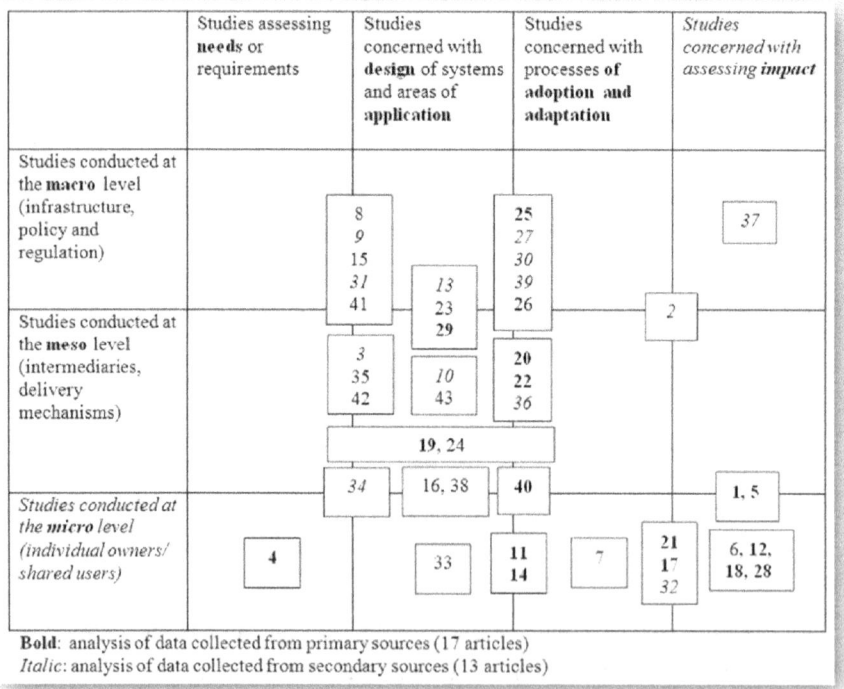

	Studies assessing **needs** or requirements	Studies concerned with **design** of systems and areas of **application**	Studies concerned with processes of **adoption and adaptation**	*Studies concerned with assessing **impact***
Studies conducted at the **macro** level (infrastructure, policy and regulation)		8 *9* 15 *31* 41	25 *27* *30* *39* 26	*37*
		13 23 29		2
Studies conducted at the **meso** level (intermediaries, delivery mechanisms)		*3* 35 42	20 22 *36*	
		10 43		
		19, 24		
	34	16, 38	40	1, 5
*Studies conducted at the **micro** level (individual owners/ shared users)*	**4**	33	11 14	7	21 *17* *32*	6, 12, 18, 28

Bold: analysis of data collected from primary sources (17 articles)
Italic: analysis of data collected from secondary sources (13 articles)

Source: [34]

In close examination of Exhibit 18, the mapping exercise shows a coalescing of studies around system design and areas of application. A large segment of this group also overlap into adoption, whilst a lesser number overlap into considering needs, and two studies span needs, design and adoption. Only one study deals exclusively with adoption and one exclusively with assessing needs. Fewer studies are found at either end of the lifecycle, with only five studies identified that make use of primary data to assess impact of m-finance initiatives at the micro level. The collection and analysis of (new) primary data is concentrated at the micro level, whilst studies at the meso and macro levels analyze some primary data sources, but a greater number of secondary.

GEOGRAPHICAL FOCUS

Research categorization can also be done by geographic focus to understand the regional/contextual distribution or representation in research.

> In Exhibit 19, the frequency of literature on e-commerce in DCs reviewed in this study fairly indicate that most of the present research of e-commerce in developing countries (published between 1993 and 2005) are concentrated in Asia, 86 articles (48%); Africa 24 articles (13%), and Latin America, 16 articles (9%).

EXHIBIT 19 DISTRIBUTIONS OF E-COMMERCE IN DCs ARTICLES BY REGION FROM 1993-2005

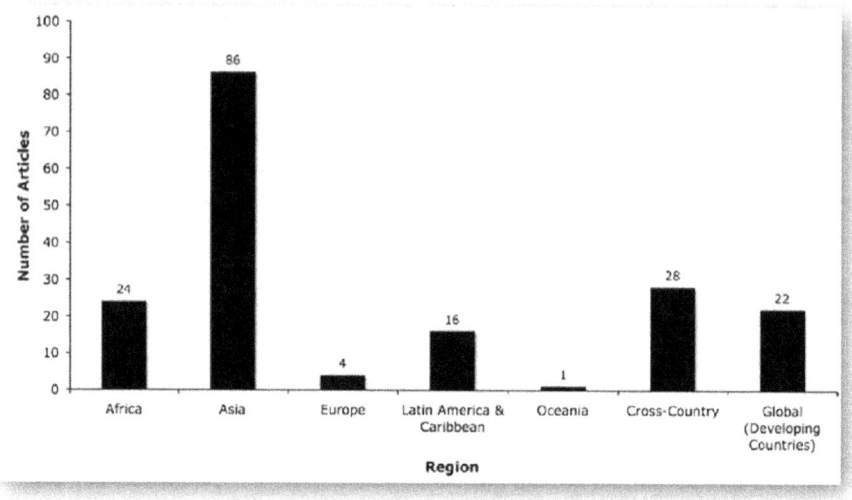

There tends to be a preponderance of Asian studies. This is arguably reflective of the relative maturity of ICT infrastructure in terms of roll-out and usage. The relative lack of literature in Latin America relates to the fact that this review was restricted to English-language journals, whereas research on Latin America is often in Spanish or Portuguese-language journals. Hence, there is still a relative under-representation of African studies on e-commerce in DCs. Within these regions, differences do occur with respect to the number of articles per country.

Perhaps the primary reason for Africa being under-researched is that academic research tends to lag in the roll-out of ICT infrastructure which is relatively lacking in countries. Hence, since ICT infrastructure has grown quite strongly post-2000 there is now the need for research to catch up.

JOURNAL

Categorization by journal tends to focus on the name of the journal (numbers) and any other key characteristics of the publication – such as Journal Ranking, Subject Area, Theme or Purpose of the Journal. Remember, the researcher conducting the LR is expected to use more than one resource, and preferably, diverse resources so that a diversity of perspectives are critically and comparatively reflected. This classification is necessary for a number of reasons. First, some journals are thematic, For example, there is a Journal of Relationship Marketing, hence, any student researching on such a theme, is required to read publications from the journal. Sometimes, some of these journals publish special issues on sub-themes related to the journal.

Second, there are also journals which have a geographic focus, For example, the Electronic Journal of Information Systems in Developing Countries tends to publish a majority of research work on information systems from a developing country perspective. Third, journals have rankings, which are sometimes questioned, but give direction to quality of research work done. Rankings are sometimes compiled by disciplinary associations like the Association of Information Systems which has a list of recognized journals that are ranked. The Association of Business Schools also has a list of Journal Rankings to guide researchers in business schools. Other researchers and research institutions also publish a journal quality list. These lists adopt different measures for ranking the journals or assessing their quality. I will briefly summarize some of these lists of recognized journals.

- The **Journal Quality List**, compiled and edited by Professor Anne-Wil Harzing, is published primarily to assist academics to target papers at journals of an appropriate standard. Whilst every effort has been made to ensure the accuracy of the Journal Quality List, the editor recommends that it be checked before being used extensively for evaluation purposes. Source: Forty-ninth Edition, published on 8 June 2013, http://www.harzing.com.

- **Association of Business Schools Journal Quality Guide**

  The ABS Academic Journal Quality Guide is a hybrid based partly upon peer review, partly upon statistical information relating to citation, and partly upon editorial judgments following from the detailed evaluation of many hundreds of publications over a long period. It provides a guide to the range, subject matter and relative quality of journals in which business and management academics might publish the results of their research. Source: Academic Journal Quality Guide, Version 4 published in March 2010 http://tinyurl.com/absjournal2010.

- **Thomson Reuters Journal Citation Guide 2011**

  Journal Citation Reports (JCR) is an annual publication by the Science and Scholarly Research division of Thomson Reuters. It offers a systematic, objective means to critically evaluate the world's leading journals, with quantifiable, statistical information based on citation data. By compiling articles' cited references, JCR helps to measure research influence and impact at the journal and category levels, and shows the relationship between citing and cited journals. Source: http://thomsonreuters.com/journal-citation-reports/ | Download 2011 List - http://tinyurl.com/jcr2011final

In my review on e-commerce in developing countries, I categorized e-commerce in DCs literature by journals to identify the number of journals covered in the review, ranking of the journals and special issues on the themes (Exhibit 20).

EXHIBIT 20 DISTRIBUTION OF E-COMMERCE IN DCS ARTICLES BY SELECTED JOURNALS

Top E-commerce Journals	Number of Articles	IS Journals focused on Global IT Issues, DCs and Development	Number of Articles
Electronic Markets	21 (11.6%)	Electronic Journal of Information Systems in Developing Countries	12 (6.6%)
Electronic Commerce Research	10 (5.5%)	Journal of Global Information Management	11 (6.1%)
Journal of Electronic Commerce Research	8 (4.4%)	Journal of Global Information Technology Management	11 (6.1%)
International Journal of Electronic Commerce	7 (3.9%)	Information Technology for Development	7 (3.9%)
Communication of AIS	2 (1.1%)	Information Technology & People	3 (1.7%)
Journal of Management Information Systems	1 (0.6%)	Information Technologies & International Development	3 (1.7%)
Information Systems Research	1 (0.6%)		
MIS Quarterly	0 (%)		
Total	50 (27.7 %)	Total	47 (26.1%)
Other Journals	131 (72.3%)	Other Journals	134 (73.9%)
Total of All Journals	181 (100%)	Total of All Journals	181 (100%)

Exhibit 20 shows the percentage of total articles by selected journals, which consist of top e-commerce journals and other IS journals focused on global IT issues, DCs and development. The fourteen selected journals contribute to slightly above 50 percent of total number of journal articles; 50 articles, 27.7%, top e-commerce journals and 47 articles, 26.1% for IS journals focused on DCs and development. The journal with the highest percentage of articles is *Electronic Markets*, which also tends to be one of the top e-commerce journals. It is a quarterly journal, first published in German between 1991 and 1993 and in English since 1993, focusing on issues including the relationship between ICT innovation, the potential value creation and the effects on organizations and society. The *Electronic Journal of Information Systems in Developing Countries* is the journal with the second largest number of articles; 12 articles (6.6%). It's been in publication since 2000, serving as an international forum for academics, practitioners and policy makers to share knowledge and experience on the development, implementation and management of IS in DCs.

The *Journal of Global Information Management* and *Journal of Global Information Technology Management* are the journals with the third (tie) largest number of articles; each having 11 articles (6.1%). They are both international journals, with the former publishing original material focused on global information and its implications on information technology, and the latter addressing international issues of IT management. Other top e-commerce journals that made a substantial contribution of articles are *Electronic Commerce Research*, 10 articles (5.5%); *Journal of Electronic Commerce Research*, 8 articles (4.4%); and the *International Journal of Electronic Commerce*, 7 articles (3.9%). These quarterly journals stimulate and disseminate research on several issues related to e-commerce including business activities, theories, applications, and technologies. The *Journal of Electronic Commerce Research* and *Electronic Commerce Research* are relatively new journals, which began publishing in 2000 and 2001 respectively. Other IS journals focused on DCs, development and global issues, that made a substantial contribution of articles is *Information Technology for Development*; 7 articles (3.9%).

Industry/Artefact/Infrastructure

Exhibit 21 Number of Articles by Infrastructure

Infrastructure		Number of Articles
Applications		114 (63%)
- Organizational Systems	29 (16%)	
- Financial Services	26 (14%)	
- Retailing	17 (9%)	
- Electronic Payment Systems	5 (3%)	
- Electronic Services	2 (2%)	
- Auctions	1 (1%)	
- Education and Training	1 (1%)	
- General Applications	33 (18%)	
Hard Infrastructure		13 (7%)
General		54 (30%)
Total		181 (100%)

Source: [31]

Depending on the nature of the topic in question, there is sometimes the need to categorize literature by some key characteristics of the topic. For example, e-commerce research can be categorized by the industry in which the research was conducted or the type of technological artifact or infrastructure researched. These categorizations may depend on the researcher's interests or purpose of the review. For example, I categorized e-commerce in DCs research by Infrastructure to better understand the technological applications employed in the existing research (Exhibit 21).

In close examination, Exhibit 21 shows that the bulk of the articles are focused on e-commerce applications or soft infrastructure, 114 articles (63%) as compared to hard infrastructure, 13 articles (7%). The less researched applications stem from research studies in Asia – China and Hong Kong – (Westland et al., 1997; Westland et al., 1998; Poon and Chau, 2001) and Latin America (Joia and Zamot, 2002; Rodriguez, 2005). None of the less researched applications were represented in other developing regions like Africa. E-commerce research in Africa centered on the use of email, and Internet for creating online presence, searching for suppliers; and providing retail and banking services (Bekele, 2000; Sørensen and Buatsi, 2002; Kamel and Hussein, 2004; Ezehoha, 2005; Molla and Licker, 2005b). In comparing developing regions, sub-Saharan Africa has 2.8 Internet users per 100 inhabitants as compared to 11.7 in Eastern Asia and 15.2 in Latin America and the Caribbean (ITU, 2007).

RESEARCH GAPS

The final category identifies key research trends and gaps relating to all or the key categories used by the researcher. These may include research issues, the theoretical and methodological approaches, and geographic focus. It is also advisable for the researcher to outline the future research directions concerning the topic in question. Exhibit 22 shows an example of research gaps outlined from my review on e-commerce in DCs research.

Exhibit 22 Research Gaps in E-commerce in DCs Research

Research Issue Gaps

What tends to be lacking in research, is firstly, a wider perspective of potential benefits of e-commerce and relative e-commerce applications that can help achieve that. Literature on e-commerce potential and constraints in DCs has particularly focused on the potential firm-level opportunities and benefits, as compared to the contribution of e-commerce to development and the means by which this may be achieved. With business-to-business activities having gained much attention from researchers, a focus on how e-commerce can impact on development, could also open more opportunities for the introduction of other consumer oriented and government/public sector-to-business e-commerce activities and the subsequent adoption of related applications and technologies including mobile commerce.

Theory Gaps

The second gap focuses on the need to develop a theoretically grounded and practically oriented understanding of how DC firms can address or navigate around the institutional constraints and challenges in their contexts to achieve the e-commerce benefits identified. As realized from the above results, much has been researched and published on adoption and diffusion, investigating the variety of factors that discriminate e-commerce adopters from non-adopters either at the firm level, sector/industry or country level. It tends to be that most literature on e-commerce in DCs have been rather silent in addressing the issue of offering strategic guidance to DC firms to handle their institutional constraints and move beyond adoption to institutionalize e-commerce into organizational routine and processes. The use of strategy related theories such as the resource-based theory and adaptation-evolution strategies of firms, in studying e-commerce research provides an opportunity to investigate how DC firms develop firm-specific capabilities within their volatile environment to support e-commerce and realize its benefits.

Methodological Gaps

Notwithstanding, this also raises other research methodological issues, emphasizing the need for more case studies and mixed methods in studying e-commerce in DCs research. Case studies enable a contemporary phenomenon like e-commerce to be studied within its real-life context, especially when the boundaries between the phenomenon and its context are not clearly evident (Yin, 1994: 13). Combining case studies with other research methods like surveys can facilitate the unearthing of underlying structures, processes and relationships observed in the quantitative description of trends, attitudes, or opinions of a population under study. This offers the opportunity to engage in theory building in research areas where relatively few prior research and theory exists, like organizational strategies of DC firms (Montealegre and Keil, 2000).

Though not exhaustive, the attempt by this review to classify the current state of e-commerce in DCs research has yielded several important implications and reasonable insights that can guide researchers in future research. More knowledge is required to enable DC firms exploit and sustain e-commerce benefits and substantially contribute to development in their contexts.

Analyzing and Writing

Two main stages are involved in analyzing the literature: evaluating the source and analyzing the source.

EVALUATING THE SOURCE

Your first line of evaluation should be to ask: "Is this item relevant: does it tell me something I need for my research paper/long essay?" If not, then reject it. If so, then continue. <u>Never</u> simply accept what is written or said. You must be critical when you assess any source. Some typical evaluation questions you can ask are:

- *Who* wrote this?
- *Why* did they write this – do they have some particular interest or 'angle' that would make them likely to present data in a particular light (e.g. a company with a financial involvement)?
- *How* did they get their data and come to their conclusions – are there any possible problems with what they have done?
- *When* did they do the work – is it up-to-date, or likely to have been superseded?
- *What* else do you know – does this support or contradict other sources of evidence?

On this last point, you should typically aim for **TRIANGULATION**: viewing an issue from various different sources, evidence types, and perspectives in order to get a balanced view. Your overall evaluation will give you a sense of how valuable, or not, the particular source is.

ANALYZING THE SOURCE

How you analyze a piece of literature depends very much on your purpose. In some cases, analysis may be fairly straightforward:

1. If you're looking for some specific item of data, e.g. how many commercial banks are in Ghana?
2. If you're looking for conceptual models that can inform your research paper, e.g. which model will explain the social determinants of internet banking adoption?

3. If you're looking for examples of the use of particular research methods to study the topic in question in a particular context, e.g. are there any quantitative studies on internet banking adoption in an African country or developing country?

SYNTHESIZING LITERATURE

Once you have completed the categorization of literature, you can begin writing your paper. When you begin to write the body of the paper, you may want to follow these steps [36]:

(1) Select one common sub-theme/argument and divide it into sub-topics that represent paragraph size "chunks." See example below:

> **Initial efforts** at finding answers to these questions can be analyzed from **two perspectives**: the <u>practitioner</u> and <u>academic research</u> perspectives. The initiatives of mobile network operators, banks, entrepreneurs, governments and development agencies characterize efforts from the <u>practitioner perspective</u>. These efforts tend to focus on the design and adoption of mobile applications for microfinance activities or to enhance access to financial services (Donner, 2008; CGAP, 2008). Efforts addressing the impact of mobiles on development concerns and needs – combating poverty and stimulating economic growth – are quite few. This imbalance is also reflected on the <u>academic research front</u> (Duncombe and Boateng, 2009). There is a preponderance of research studies documenting the business models which characterize the initial efforts of practitioners, mobile operators and banks. Academics have begun to catch up with studies seeking development solutions through mobile phones (Heeks and Jagun, 2008; Donner, 2010; Zuckerman, 2010).

(2) For each "chunk" create a topic sentence that (1) synthesizes the literature to be discussed, and (2) describes the literature to be discussed. Here are some examples of topic sentences:

- These efforts tend to focus on the design and adoption of mobile applications for micro-finance activities or to enhance access to financial services (Donner, 2008; CGAP, 2008).
  - *The first highlighted section synthesizes the literature; the second highlighted section describes the literature.*
- There is a preponderance of research studies documenting the business models which characterize the initial efforts of practitioners, mobile operators and banks.
  - *The first highlighted section synthesizes the literature; the second highlighted section describes the literature.*

(3) Support the topic sentences you created in #2 with quotes, paraphrases and references from/on the source material. As you incorporate source material, make sure to use clear transitions that relate the sources to each other and to your topic sentences.

- Academics have begun to catch up with studies seeking development solutions through mobile phones (Heeks and Jagun, 2008; Donner, 2010; Zuckerman, 2010).

Adhering to the above three steps will enable the researcher to be able to develop arguments, and support them with appropriate references as evidence, and with illustrations to enhance understanding. Literature review is about **argument (what is the view), evidence (source of the view)** and **illustrations (examples to show that the view exists)**.

In Exhibit 23, the underlined sentences are the arguments, the highlighted references are the evidence and the phrases in bold are the illustrations being used to support the arguments.

Exhibit 23 Social Networking in the Workplace

Social networking is increasingly becoming a phenomenon in the social and business lifestyles of employees.

Statistics from the 2011 Forbes report on Social networking and business stated that, 85 per cent of workers in America spend a minimum of 30 minutes of working hours to visit social networking websites (Forbes, 2011). These statistics are **not too far** from that of Africans, as a recent study in South Africa also found that 70 per cent of South African workers interviewed browsed Facebook during working hours (Ngu, 2011). Then again, beyond the concern on growth in the use of social networking platforms in the workplace, there have been concerns about the implications it has on both employers and employees (Jackson, 2012). While **some employers have been** reported to be requesting access passwords to employee accounts (California Times, 2012); **others are exploring** policies and strategies to leverage social media in marketing and sales (Carmen, 2009; BBC, 2011).

Somehow businesses have to respond to this growing phenomenon. However, the questions are should employers be concerned - what are the potential risks and benefits of social networking in the workplace and how can businesses address these risks?

PICTURE 1 LITERATURE REVIEW SNAPSHOT

A literature review IS NOT:

- A summary of available materials without any critical description or component: or
- An annotated bibliography

Argument/View and Evidence

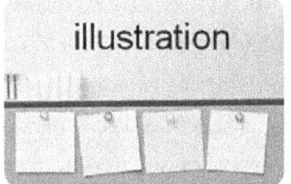

illustration

Writing a Literature Review

Literature review - a product or a process

Before we discuss writing a LR, it is important to explain some frequent misconceptions of LR. LR can be considered as both a product and a process. As a product, LR is viewed as the output of the process of writing a review. For example, every research paper or dissertation or long essay has a section usually known as the literature review. Thus, a research paper or long essay will contain a literature review as one of its parts. In this scenario the literature is used as a foundation for a new insight or argument developed by the researcher. This said, it is also important to note that, throughout the process of writing a research paper or long essay, a researcher will need to summarize and synthesize arguments from others. Hence, beyond the section called LR, there are several other sections, technically almost throughout the paper or long essay, that some level of reviewing of literature may be required. The only thing that changes is the purpose of the review. The purpose of reviewing literature in the introduction will differ from the analysis or conclusion. Consequently, LR as a process is the act of identifying, categorizing, evaluating, synthesizing and writing the review.

Organizing the Literature review

Literature reviews also must contain at least three basic elements [37]: an introduction or background information section; the body of the review containing the discussion of sources; and, finally, a conclusion and/or recommendations section to end the LR paper.

- *Introduction:* Gives a brief introduction of the topic of the literature review, such as the central theme or organizational pattern.
- *Body:* Contains your discussion of sources and is organized chronologically, thematically, or methodologically.
- *Conclusions/Recommendations:* Discuss what you have drawn from reviewing literature so far. Where might the discussion proceed?

Chronological Review

Chronological reviews present the literature according to when they were published. For example, if researchers' views have tended to change over time, the review will show a clear trend or changes in trends. The extract below is an example of a chronological review. The first sentence is an opening sentence introducing the topic to be discussed or reviewed. The last sentence presents the summary or the take away from reviewing the literature so far. In between the first and last sentences, the author conducts a chronological review of factors which contribute to unemployment in Africa.

> Literature demonstrates that the key factors which contribute to unemployment in Africa have tended to change over time. In the late 1990's researchers argued that inflation and low wages contributed to unemployment (Uche, 2000; Benson, 2003). For example a study by Uche (2000) on unemployment in the banking industry in Nigeria highlighted that inflation affected the turnover of banks, which had also had an effect on salary payments. Over 2000 bank employees lost their jobs by the end of 1999.
>
> On the other hand, by 2004, researchers discussed that lack of capital for start-up initiatives and high interest rates on loans stalled entrepreneurial ventures and contributed to unemployment or the lack of job opportunities (Thakur, 2005). A comparative study (Kinson, 2006) on the SME industry in Ghana and Uganda shared similar findings on the effects of start-up capital and interest loans on entrepreneurship and unemployment. In a recent study on unemployment in Egypt, Salia (2011) found political instability, poor governance and lack of foreign direct investment to be the critical factors influencing unemployment. Other studies in Cote d'Ivoire and Sierra Leone attest to these findings (Johnson, 2009; Pern, 2010).
>
> In effect, unemployment in Africa may be viewed from a multi-facet perspective. It cannot be reduced to one single factor.

Thematic Review

In thematic review the emphasis is on the topic or issue and not necessarily on time. The review may be used to either explain the topic or discuss the key arguments posited in literature concerning the theme. The extract below is a thematic review which seeks to briefly explain the transaction cost theory.

Transaction cost theory is arguably the most commonly used theory in studying issues relating to assessment of the impact of information and communication technologies (ICTs) on commerce or trade (Pare, 2003; Milgrom and Roberts, 1992). Transaction costs, described as "the costs of running a system" (Williamson, 1985: 19), consist of two types of costs: coordination costs and actor motivation costs (Williamson, 1981; Milgrom and Roberts, 1992). Coordination entails all the information and communication related costs before, during and after a transaction. This includes the cost of searching for products, services, sellers, and buyers, and negotiating and ensuring contract compliance and post-contractual agreements (Benjamin and Wigand, 1995; Wigand *et al.*, 1997). Actor motivation costs entail the costs of having incomplete or asymmetrical information and imperfect commitment in a transaction. These costs affect decision-making and enforcement of compliance mechanisms, and contribute to the loss of contracts and contractual disputes (Pare, 2003; Milgrom and Roberts, 1992). It is suggestive from the transaction cost perspective that trading is primarily about information. It involves the sharing and communication of information which leads to the exchange of goods and services, and the management of relationships between parties involved. Hence, participants in a transaction seek for innovative ways to minimize costs in acquiring, accessing and communicating information for pre-trade, during-trade and post-trade activities (Williamson, 1985).

Methodological Review

Methodological reviews focus on the "methods" of the researcher or writer. The extract below discusses the research methods used in four studies on e-commerce in developing countries.

We observe the use of both quantitative and qualitative methods to study e-commerce in DCs from the resource-based theory (RBT) perspective. However, only one study (Montealegre, 2002) tends to have conducted in-depth case research on e-commerce strategy (adoption and implementation) at the firm-level. The author argues that the use of case study as a research method offers the opportunity to "engage in theory building in an area where relatively little prior research has been conducted" (Benbasat *et al.*, 1987 cited in Montealegre, 2002: 516). It also allows the study of this phenomenon – e-commerce in DC firms – in its natural setting. The potential contributory value of case research is therefore emphasized vis-à-vis the path-dependency of resource development (Montealgre, 2002) and the non-universality of sources of creating and sustaining firm performance (Barney, 1997). Consequently, future research seeking to develop a process-based model of resource development may benefit from this research method to build the application of RBT in e-commerce in DCs and provide the related strategic insight to DC firms.

Structuring a Literature Review As a Chapter/Paper

There is no one best method for structuring a literature review as a chapter in a long essay or as a research paper. The approaches may differ depending on the purpose of the review. Some reviews seek to take stock of existing literature and review to determine research gaps and directions for future research. This type of review is a good starting point for research students (PhD or MPhil) since it provides a solid foundation to determine research gaps and justify the research purpose. It may be quite detailed for a non-research based graduate program. Non-research graduate students can develop their literature review with a purpose of explaining the concepts in the research topic and developing a research framework to address the research question.

An outline for a review which could be done by a non-research graduate student is presented in Exhibit 24 and that for a research graduate student is presented in Exhibit 25. Reviews for the non-research graduate students' dissertation or long essay are usually thematic; focusing on explaining the concepts which underpin the topic and reviewing literature which directly address the research questions. However, for the research graduate student, the LR may need to focus on establishing research gaps to clearly justify the potential knowledge contribution. As such, the review may need to be extensive, covering almost all the classification categories discussed earlier. It is like establishing what we know and what we don't know about the topic in question.

EXHIBIT 24 SAMPLE OUTLINES OF A LITERATURE REVIEW (NON-RESEARCH GRADUATE STUDENT)

Chapter 2 Knowledge and Learning in Organizations

2.1 What is Knowledge?
    2.1.1 Tacit and Explicit Knowledge
    2.1.2 Individual and Collective Knowledge
2.2 How Learning Occurs
    2.2.1 Learning in the Individual/Employee
    2.2.2 Learning in the Organization
    2.2.3 Defining Organizational Learning

2.3   Facilitating Learning: Organizational Learning Cycle
      2.3.1   The Role of Culture
2.4   Summary

EXHIBIT 25 OUTLINE OF A DETAILED LITERATURE REVIEW (RESEARCH GRADUATE STUDENT)

Sample Papers to read are: [30] [31] [34]

ABSTRACT

A.   Introduction/Background and Rationale for the Review

B.   Framing XXXX Research

   B1. XXXXX Defined

   B2. Description of Concepts

   B3. Classification of XXXX Research

C1. Methodology for the Literature Review

C2. Presentation of Findings

   C2a. Distribution of Articles in Top Journals in your discipline

   C2b. Distribution of Articles by Year

   C2c. Distribution of Business Activities/Stakeholders

   C2d. Distribution of Research Focus (Sub-Themes may be included)

D.   Mapping XXXXX Research: Issues and Evidence

   •   Mapping of Articles Reviewed According Issues and Level of Analysis

   D1. Sub-theme 1

   D2. Sub-theme 2

   D3. Sub-theme 3

   D4. Sub-theme 4

E.   Conceptual Approaches and Methodological Issues in XXXX Research

   E1. Conceptual Approaches

      •   Mapping of Articles according to Conceptual and Methodological Approaches Taken

      •   Mapping Conceptual Approaches to XXXX

E2. Methodological Issues
- Mapping of Articles according to Methodological Approaches Taken

E3. Geographical Distribution
- Distribution of XXXX Research by Geographical Location
- Mapping of Articles Africa/DCs according Issues and Level of Analysis

F.   Research Gaps and Future Research Directions
- F1. Gaps in Issues and Evidence
- F2. Gaps in Conceptual Approach
- F3. Gaps in Methodological Approach
- F4. Conclusions and Pointers for Future Research

G. References

G1. Previous Literature Reviews Concerning XXXXX

G2. Research Articles Included in the Review

Summary

LR provides a detailed synthesis of a research topic from the perspective of existing literature, and, further, critique, compare and propose perspectives or directions of addressing the research gaps identified. LR can be viewed either as a product or the output of the process of writing a review or can be viewed as a process of identifying, categorizing, evaluating, synthesizing and writing the review.

The steps for conducting and writing a LR have been discussed. The takeaway is the need for the researcher to be able to select relevant materials and resources on the topic in question, synthesize and critically evaluate and compare them to write a good review.

In the next chapter we will discuss literature referencing.

Chapter Discussions

Mobiles and Micro-Trading: Conceptualizing the Link

There has been a tremendous growth in mobile phone ownership and use globally. Statistics from the International Telecommunication Union tend to suggest that mobile phone subscribers currently constitute 60 percent of the world population (ITU, 2008a). The rapid diffusion of this relatively low-cost technology has spurred a development agenda questioning how mobile phones can be harnessed more effectively for socio-economic development in developing economies and other resource-poor contexts.

Initial efforts in finding answers to these questions can be analyzed from two perspectives: the practitioner and academic research perspectives. The initiatives of mobile network operators, banks, entrepreneurs, governments and development agencies characterize efforts from the practitioner perspective. These efforts tend to focus on the design and adoption of mobile applications for micro-finance activities or to enhance access to financial services (Donner, 2008; CGAP, 2008). Efforts addressing the impact of mobiles on development concerns and needs – combating poverty and stimulating economic growth – are quite few. This imbalance is also reflected on the academic research front (Duncombe and Boateng, 2009). There is a preponderance of research studies documenting the business models which characterize the initial efforts of practitioners, mobile operators and banks. Academics have begun to catch up with studies seeking development solutions through mobile phones (Heeks and Jagun, 2008; Donner, 2010; Zuckerman, 2010). Some of the few studies making strides at correcting the imbalance argue that there are complexities of factors which affect the poor and hence, make it challenging for researchers to conceptualize the associated needs and impact of mobile phones with one theoretical model or theory (Aminuzzaman et al., 2003). This often contributes to the blurred distinctions between amplification and transformational effects, and also between social and production (business) spheres in adoption and usage (Donner, 2007). Thus, future studies will have to draw on a more comprehensive approach to evaluate the multi-stranded impact of mobile phones on the livelihoods of adopters.

This paper responds to this call for research. The paper investigates the impact of mobile phones on the micro-trading activities of women traders in Ghana. Extant literature has fairly covered studies on the mobile phone's usage and mobiles for development in sub-Saharan Africa. The studies include mobile phones and fisherman and farmers in Ghana (Boadi et al., 2007); mobile phone sharing practices in Ghana (Sey, 2009); mobile phones and development in Nigeria (Heeks and Jagun, 2007; Jagun et al., 2008); mobile payments in Uganda (Duncombe, 2009) and mobile phone ownership and social capital in Tanzania and South Africa (Goodman, 2005). Despite these studies, there is a call for more studies to test earlier findings in different contexts and in different micro-economic activities in order to contribute to a better understanding of the impact of mobile phones in developing economies. The underpinning research question is: what is the impact of mobile phones on the micro-trading activities of women traders in Ghana?

Source: [19]

QUESTION 1

In relation to the definition of literature review, outline the first three steps of literature review and explain how the author (of the above research problem) followed the first three steps to write the above research problem.

CHAPTER 4

Literature Referencing

Objectives

This chapter provides direction to researchers on how to provide references for arguments used in their write-ups.

Literature Referencing

IN WRITING A research manuscript, one must not forget to acknowledge any thoughts and ideas from other works that have influenced the conduct, interpretation and conclusions of the manuscript. This is usually done by including a citation of the work in the body, and its corresponding literature reference in the list of references section of the paper. This chapter aims to outline how to reference using the Harvard and American Psychological Association (APA) styles of referencing, both in-text and in the list of references.

All statements, opinions and conclusions among others that a researcher captures from another writer's work must be acknowledged, whether the work is directly quoted, paraphrased or summarized. **The act of acknowledging these various works is referred to as Literature referencing, and consists of two main elements, namely:** references within the text and a list of references produced at the end of the manuscript.

TYPES OF REFERENCING

Several literature referencing styles exist. A style refers to a set of rules that point out how a reference should be given, as well as how the various elements in a reference should be provided, in relation to each other. There are different traditions for the use of different styles in different study programs, journals and institutions. Hence one must check the target of the manuscript in order to determine the appropriate referencing style to adopt. However, two styles, the Harvard and APA styles, are discussed in this chapter. The Harvard style is based on an author-year system, in which the surname of the author (s) and the year of publication are mentioned within the text itself. While in the reference list the full reference is given in alphabetical order. It is mainly used in the social sciences, technology and the natural sciences, and at the same time serves as a foundation for other referencing styles. One of such referencing styles is the APA style, which is based on the Harvard system and is frequently used in the social sciences and the humanities. But, remember that once a particular style is chosen, it must be used consistently throughout the entire manuscript.

APA Rules for In-text Referencing

QUOTES

A short quotation of fewer than 40 words should be integrated into the text and placed within quotation marks. The name of the author, the year and the number of the page where the quote can be located should also be put in brackets directly after the quote.

For example: "Knowledge – intensity and dispersion – may be viewed as a transaction characteristic which can influence the achievement of transaction benefits" (Boateng, 2011, p. 59).

A quotation of 40 or more words should be set as a separate paragraph by the use of a block quotation, without quotation marks. Similarly, the author's name, year and page number should be placed in brackets directly after the quote.

For example

As a theoretically-based approach located in the field of economics, the conceptual framework therefore enables practitioner-researchers to analyze the needs of the target "entity", explore their mobile phone adoption and usage patterns in trading activities, and assess outcome/benefits and impact. For example, traders exist in different categories – iterant trader, wholesaler, retailer, and street hawker – and trade in different goods and services. (Boateng, 2011, p. 59)

REFERENCES

Several publications in the same year by the same author or group of authors are indicated by placing a, b, c, etc. after the year.

For example: There has been a tremendous growth in mobile phone ownership and use globally. Statistics from the International Telecommunication Union tend to suggest that mobile phone subscribers currently constitute 60 percent of the world population (ITU, 2008a). In countries like Ghana, it is estimated that there are 50 mobile phone subscriptions per 100 inhabitants, and further, the ratio of mobile cellular sub-scriptions to fixed telephone lines is 80 to one (ITU, 2008b).

When using secondary sources, the writer must name the source and give the secondary source quote.

For example: Boateng & Boateng (2008) (quoted in Hinson, 2012)

If a source has no author or if the author is anonymous, the writer must give the title's first words and the year. The title of an article or chapter is indicated using quotation marks, whereas the title of books, brochures or reports is written in italics.

For example: "Corporate Social Responsibility reportage on bank websites in Ghana" (2010)

For publications with multiple authors which are referred to several times in the text:

- 2 authors: The writer must name both authors each time the reference is quoted.
    For example: Boateng & Boateng (2008) or (Boateng & Boateng, 2008)
- 3, 4 or 5 authors: The writer must name all the authors the first time he quotes them, and from then on use only the surname of the lead author, followed by *et al.*
    For example: Hinson, Boateng & Madichie (2010), followed by Hinson *et al.* (2010)
- 6 or more authors: The writer must only give the lead author's surname, followed by *et al.*
    For example: Boateng *et al.* (2013)

Richard Boateng

Harvard Rules for In-text Referencing

QUOTES

Quotes consisting of two to three lines or less must be integrated into the text and placed in quotation marks. The name of the author, year and number of the page where the quote can be located must be put in brackets after the quote.

For example: "Knowledge – intensity and dispersion – may be viewed as a transaction characteristic which can influence the achievement of transaction benefits" (Boateng, 2011, p. 59).

If the quote is more than two to three lines, it must be placed in an indented paragraph, with no quotation marks. Similarly, the name of the author, year and number of the page where the quote can be located must be put in brackets after the quote.

For example

As a theoretically-based approach located in the field of economics, the conceptual framework therefore enables practitioner-researchers to analyze the needs of the target "entity", explore their mobile phone adoption and usage patterns in trading activities, and assess outcome/benefits and impact. For example, traders exist in different categories – iterant trader, wholesaler, retailer, and street hawker – and trade in different goods and services. (Boateng, 2011, p. 59)

REFERENCES

Multiple publications by the same author in the same year should be distinguished by placing a, b, c, etc. after the year.

For example: There has been a tremendous growth in mobile phone ownership and use globally. Statistics from the International Telecommunication Union tend to suggest that mobile phone subscribers currently constitute 60 percent of the world population (ITU, 2008a). In countries like Ghana, it is estimated that there are 50 mobile phone subscriptions per 100 inhabitants, and further, the ratio of mobile cellular subscriptions to fixed telephone lines is 80 to one (ITU, 2008b).

If a reference has more than two authors the writer must only give the surname of the lead author, followed by *et al.*

For example: Abor *et al.* (2010)

If a source has no identifiable author, the writer must use the title and the year.

For example: "Corporate Social Responsibility reportage on bank websites in Ghana" (2010)

When using secondary sources, the writer must name the source and give a quote for the secondary source.

For example: In 1987, Smith (cited in Jones, 2000 p. 3) discovered that the entire

DOCUMENTS WITHOUT YEAR OF PUBLICATION

Written sources without a year of publication can be cited by using the abbreviation s.a., which is latin for sine anno meaning without year.

For example: Boateng (s.a. p. 5)

Producing a List of References

A list of references is a list of all the sources the writer has referred to in the entire manuscript. It must be written such that it contains enough information for the researcher or a third party to be able to trace the item to a scholarly source. It is pertinent for a researcher to be consistent in terms of referencing style, and precise when citing references. The same set of rules that apply in the chosen style of referencing, should be followed every time the researcher cites a reference both in-text and in the list of references. Furthermore, all the references should be listed in alphabetical order at the end of the paper or dissertation. The list of references is often followed by a bibliography, which is a separate list of sources which the writer read but did not refer to, as well as a list of the sources which are relevant to your topic.

PRODUCING A LIST OF REFERENCES IN THE HARVARD STYLE

In producing a list of references in the Harvard style the researcher needs to remember to indent on the second and subsequent lines in each reference, as well as the following:

- To arrange the list alphabetically according to the surnames of the lead authors
- To use 'and' before the last author, if there are 2 to 7 authors
- To use italics or underline titles of journals and book titles
- To start the list of references on a new page

Books
Surname of lead author, Initial(s) (Year) *Book title in italics*. Edition - if available. Place: Publisher.

For example: Milgrom, P. and Roberts, J. (2002) *Economics, Organization, and Management*. 2nd edn. Englewood Cliffs, NJ: Prentice Hall.

Online books
Surname of lead author, Initial(s) (Year) *Book title in italics*. Publisher [Online]. Available at: URL (Accessed: Date)

For example: Bick, J. (2000) *101 Thing You Need To Know about Internet Law.* Ebrary [Online]. Available at: http://site.ebrary.com/lib/ntnu/ (Accessed: 30th March 2004).

Anthology (books with articles)
An anthology is a book with one editor, but where the chapters are written by several different authors.

Surname of lead author, Initial(s) (Year) 'Title of chapter', in Last name of editor, Initial(s) (ed.) *Book title in italics.* Edition. Place: Publisher, page.

For example: Beizer, J.L. and Timiras, M.L. (1994) 'Pharmacology and drug management in the elderly', in Timiras, P.S. (ed.) *Physiological basis of aging and geriatrics.* 2nd edn. Boca Raton: CRC Press, pp. 279-284.

Journal articles
Surname of lead author, Initial(s) and Surname (s), Initial(s) of other author (s) (Year) 'Title of article', *Title of journal in italics,* volume (issue), page.

For example: Duncombe, R. and Boateng, R. (2009) 'Mobile phones and financial services in developing countries: a review of concepts, methods, issues, evidence and future research directions', *Third World Quarterly,* 30(7), pp. 1237-1258.

Online journal articles
Surname of lead author, Initial(s) and Surname (s) of other author (s), Initial(s) (Year) 'Title of article', *Title of journal in italics,* volume (issue), page. [Online] Available at: URL (Accessed: Date)

For example: Grönroos, C. (1994) 'Keynote paper: From marketing mix to relationship marketing - towards a paradigm shift in marketing', *Management Decision,* 32(2), pp. 4-20 [Online] Available at: http://faculty.mu.edu.sa/public/uploads/1361463356.303marketing%20 mix2.pdf (Accessed: 29th December 2004).

Conference papers
Unpublished papers:
Surname of author, Initial(s) (Year) *Title of paper in italics*. Unpublished paper presented at Name of conference. Place.

For example: Okai, L.S. (2013) *Developing a Strategic Model for Online Relationship Marketing*. Unpublished paper presented at UGBS Conference on Business and Development, April 8-9. Accra, Ghana.

Published papers:
Surname of author, Initial(s) (Year) 'Title of paper', in Surname of editor, Initial(s) (ed.) *Title of conference in italics*. Place: Publisher, page.

For example: Nørvåg, K. (2003) 'Space-efficient support for temporal text indexing in a document archive context', in Koch, T. and Sølvberg, I. (ed.) *Research and Advanced Technology for Digital Libraries, 7th European Conference, ECDL 2003, Trondheim, Norway, August 17-22, 2003*. Berlin: Springer, pp. 511-522.

Newspapers and popular magazines
Surname, Initial(s) (Year) 'Title of article', *Title of newspaper in italics*, Date, page.

For example: Appiah, S. (2014) 'Roast plantain business thrives', *Daily Graphic*, 1st February 2014, p. 11.

Web page
Author (Year) *Title in italics*. Available at: URL (Accessed: Date).

For example: Ciotti, G. (2013) *The Business Case for Building Real Relationships with Customers*. Available at: https://www.helpscout.net/blog/relationship-marketing/ (Accessed: 23rd June 2013)

Web page with no authors
Title in italics (Year) Available at: URL (Accessed: Date).

For example: *The Business Case for Building Real Relationships with Customers* (2013) Available at: https://www.helpscout.net/blog/relationship-marketing/ (Accessed: 23rd June 2013)

EXAMPLE OF A LIST OF REFERENCES IN THE HARVARD STYLE

Beizer, J.L. and Timiras, M.L. (1994) 'Pharmacology and drug management in the elderly', in Timiras, P.S. (ed.) *Physiological basis of aging and geriatrics*. 2nd edn. Boca Raton: CRC Press, pp. 279-284.

Bick, J. (2000) *101 Thing You Need To Know about Internet Law*. Ebrary [Online]. Available at: http://site.ebrary.com/lib/ntnu/ (Accessed: 30th March 2004).

Duncombe, R. and Boateng, R. (2009) 'Mobile phones and financial services in developing countries: a review of concepts, methods, issues, evidence and future research directions', *Third World Quarterly*, 30(7), pp. 1237-1258.

Grönroos, C. (1994) 'Keynote paper: From marketing mix to relationship marketing - towards a paradigm shift in marketing', *Management Decision*, 32(2), pp. 4-20.

Milgrom, P. and Roberts, J. (2002) *Economics, Organization, and Management*. 2nd edn. Englewood Cliffs, NJ: Prentice Hall.

Producing a list of references in the APA style

In producing a list of references in the APA style, the researcher needs to remember to indent on the second and subsequent lines in each reference, as well as the following:

- To arrange the list alphabetically according to the surnames of the lead authors
- To use '&' before the last author if there are 2 to 7 authors
- When there are 8 or more authors, include the first 6, then insert three ellipses, and add the last author. **For example**: Krishnan, K. J., Reeve, A. K., Samuels, D. C., Chinnery, P. F., Blackwood, J. K., Taylor, R. W., . . . Turnbull, D. M.
- To use italics for the titles of journals and volumes numbers, as well as book titles
- To use indents on the second and subsequent lines in a reference
- To start the reference list on a new page.

BOOKS
Surname of lead author, Initial(s). (Year). *Book title in italics* (Edition - if available). Place: Publisher.

For example: Milgrom, P., & Roberts, J. (2002). *Economics, Organization, and Management.* (2nd edn). Englewood Cliffs, NJ: Prentice Hall.

ONLINE BOOKS
Surname of lead author, Initial(s) (Year) *Book title in italics.* Retrieved from: URL

For example: Faint, J. (2000) *Conditions for Service in the Nigerian Army.* Retrieved from: http://site.ebrary.com/lib/ntnu/

ANTHOLOGY (BOOK WITH ARTICLES)
Surname of lead author, Initial(s). (Year). Title of chapter. In Initial(s) Surname editor (Ed.), *Book title in italics* (Edition, page). Place: Publisher.

For example: Beizer, J.L., & Timiras, M.L. (1994). Pharmacology and drug management in the elderly. In P.S. Timiras (Ed.), *Physiological basis of Aging and Geriatrics* (2nd ed., pp.279-284). Boca Raton: CRC Press.

JOURNAL ARTICLES

Surname of lead author, Initial(s)., & Surname (s) of other author (s), Initial(s). (Year). Title of article. *Title of journal in italics, volume in italics* (issue), page.

For example: Duncombe, R., & Boateng, R. (2009). Mobile phones and financial services in developing countries: a review of concepts, methods, issues, evidence and future research directions. *Third World Quarterly*, 30(7), 1237-1258.

CONFERENCE PAPERS

Unpublished papers:
Surname (s) of author (s), Initial(s). (Year, Month). *Title of paper in italics*. Paper presented at Name of conference, Place.

For example: Okai, L.S. (2013, April) *Developing a Strategic Model for Online Relationship Marketing*. Paper presented at UGBS Conference on Business and Development, Accra, Ghana.

Published papers:
Surname of author, Initial(s). (Year). Title of paper. In Initial(s) Surname of editor (Ed.), *Title of conference in italics* (page). Place: Publisher.

For example: Nørvåg, K. (2003). Space-efficient support for temporal text indexing in a document archive context. In T. Koch, & I. Sølvberg (Ed.), *Research and Advanced Technology for Digital Libraries, 7th European Conference, ECDL 2003, Trondheim, Norway (pp. 511-522)*. Berlin: Springer.

NEWSPAPERS AND POPULAR MAGAZINES

Surname, Initial(s). (Year, Date). Title of article. *Title of newspaper in italics*, page.

For example: Appiah, S. (2014, 1ˢᵗ February). Roast plantain business thrives. *Daily Graphic*, p. 11.

WEB PAGE
Surname of author, Initial(s). (Year). *Title in italics*. Retrieved: Date, Year, from URL

For example: Ciotti, G. (2013). *The Business Case for Building Real Relationships with Customers*. Retrieved: 23rd June 2013, from
https://www.helpscout.net/blog/relationship-marketing/

WEB PAGES WITH NO AUTHORS
Title of article/page. (Year). Retrieved Date, Year, from URL

For example: The Business Case for Building Real Relationships with Customers. (2013). Retrieved 23ʳᵈ June, 2013, from
https://www.helpscout.net/blog/relationship-marketing/

EXAMPLE OF A LIST OF REFERENCES IN THE APA STYLE

Appiah, S. (2014, 1ˢᵗ February). Roast plantain business thrives, *Daily Graphic*, p. 11.

Beizer, J.L., & Timiras, M.L. (1994). Pharmacology and drug management in the elderly. In P.S. Timiras (Ed.), *Physiological basis of Aging and Geriatrics* (2nd ed., pp. 279-284). Boca Raton: CRC Press.

Duncombe, R., & Boateng, R. (2009). Mobile phones and financial services in developing countries: a review of concepts, methods, issues, evidence and future research directions. *Third World Quarterly, 30*(7), 1237-1258.

Nørvåg, K. (2003). Space-efficient support for temporal text indexing in a document archive context. In T. Koch, & I. Sølvberg (Ed.), *Research and Advanced Technology for Digital Libraries, 7th European Conference, ECDL 2003, Trondheim, Norway (pp. 511-522)*. Berlin: Springer.

How to Use Microsoft Word for Referencing

Though there are quite a number of software packages to manage citations and referencing in academic writing (see EndNote and Reference Manager), Microsoft Word, one of the most popular desktop applications, tends to be an equally easy to use software package which offers such features for both academics and students.

The Microsoft (MS) Word 2010's reference function is a good productivity tool to manage citations and bibliography. This section will provide guidelines in using MS Word 2010 to create a reference list [38].

CREATING REFERENCES

Microsoft Reference function is accessible from the reference tab.

PICTURE 2 REFERENCING WITH MS WORD 2010 – STEP 1

MS Word 2010 comes with a list of default referencing style. Choose the referencing style that you want to use.

PICTURE 3 REFERENCING WITH MS WORD 2010 – STEP 2

Click on the 'Insert Citation' button to open the add citation window. MS Word 2010 allows users to add different source type such as 'Journal Article' by clicking on "Add New Source". Users can also click on "Manage Sources" and click on "New…" to add a new source.

PICTURE 4 REFERENCING WITH MS WORD 2010 – STEP 3

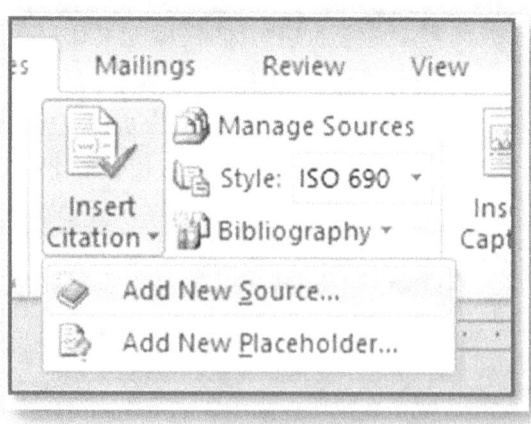

Select the type of source and begin to fill in the Bibliographic information for the source.

PICTURE 5 REFERENCING WITH MS WORD 2010 – STEP 4

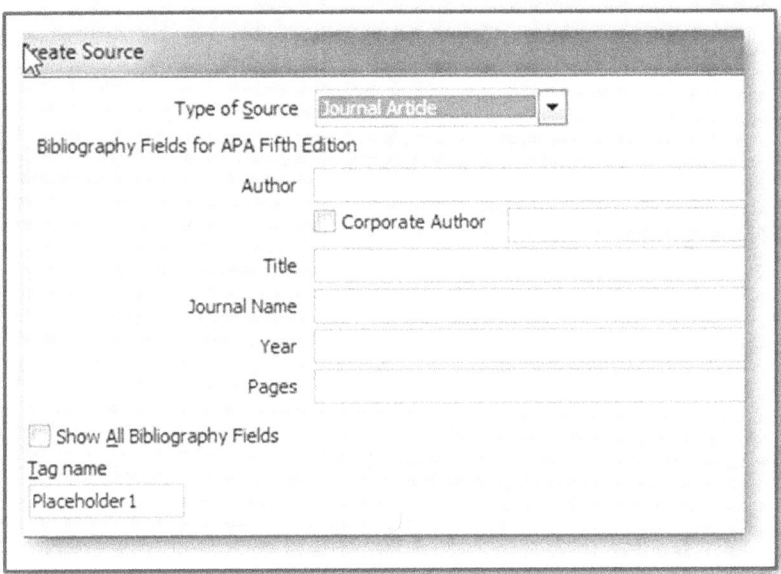

Click on the insert citation button to view a list of citations and click any of them to create an in-text citation in the research paper.

PICTURE 6 REFERENCING WITH MS WORD 2010 – STEP 5

You can create a bibliography or list of references (Works Cited) page by clicking on the 'Bibliography' button.

Picture 7 Referencing with MS Word 2010 – Step 6

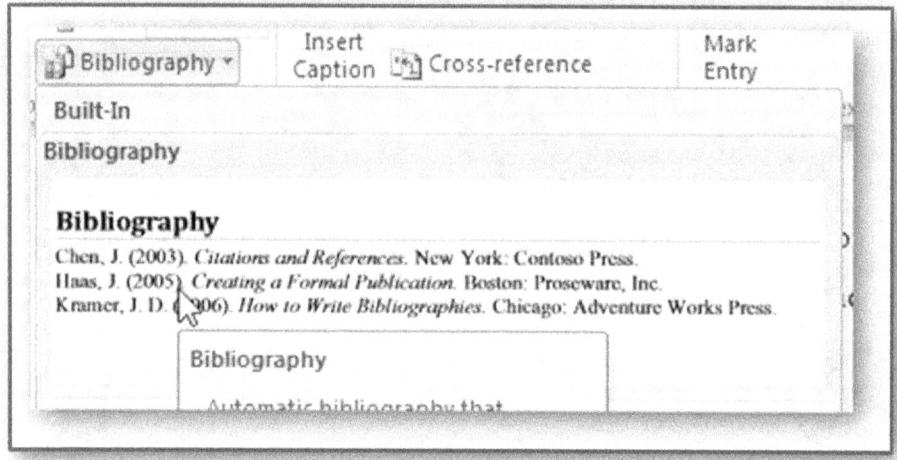

Summary

This chapter has explained the basics of referencing using the Harvard and APA referencing styles. There is also more information to be obtained through online websites. Hence, to learn more about these referencing styles, researchers can refer to:

1. For Harvard style. Please refer to:
   - http://tinyurl.com/harvardrefstyle
2. For APA style. Please refer to:
   - http://tinyurl.com/aparefstyle

In the next chapter we will discuss theoretical and conceptual approaches in research.

Chapter Discussions

Financing Behavior of Small and Medium Enterprises – Evidence from Ghana

The scholarly literature concerned with the financing behavior of business concerns, including that of small and medium-sized enterprises (SMEs), has for some time shown interest in the influence industry may have on funding choices. In the simplest terms, it has been conjectured that firms within a particular industry tend to adopt a similar financing pattern that essentially represents a consensus on what is appropriate given prevailing circumstances in the industry. Holmes *et al.* (2003, p. 112) have recently summarized extant knowledge on this matter, with emphasis on SMEs, as follows: Industry as an explanatory variable is supported by the equilibrium theory of capital structure which suggests "the economic sector a company belongs to can be an important factor ... when explaining ... financial behavior". (Lopez-Garcia & Aybar-Arias, 2000, p. 57).

(Romano, 2002) notes that sectors with strong tangible asset holdings are expected to have higher average debt levels than is evident in sectors associated with intangible or risky assets. However, there has been controversy and debate concerning the association between industry and debt structure (Jordan, Lowe & Taylor, 1998, p. 3). This debate has ranged from comments suggesting differences across industries but consistency within industries (Harris and Raviv, 1991), to claims that industry is not as important as firm-specific aspects (Balakrishnan & Fox, 1993). Jordan, Lowe and Taylor (1998) support this latter view, while Cassar and Holmes (2001), Hall, Hutchinson and Michaelas (2000), Romano, Tanewski and Smyrnios (2001), and Bennett and Donnelly (1993) find some support for an association.

Apart from highlighting that the issue of whether industry influences financing behavior is, as yet, unsettled, this quotation raises the possibility that industry is simply a proxy for one or more firm-specific characteristics that are the real underlying determinants of funding choices (Van Auken and Neely, 1996; Gibson R., 2002). These characteristics could include enterprise size, business age, profitability, growth, asset structure and risk.

In the *2012/2013* academic year, a student presented the above research problem to his supervisor. Using the above research problem answer the following question 1 below.

QUESTION 1

Explain the concept of referencing and identify three errors in the presentation of references in the above research problem.

CHAPTER 5

Theory in research

Objectives

This chapter explains the relevance of theoretical and conceptual frameworks, and theorizing in a research work[4].

---

4 Thinking about theory - degreesfiction.wordpress.com

What is a Theory?

THE DEFINITION OF theory can be taken from different perspectives, depending on the objective of the definition. In terms of its consistent elements or components, a theory can be conceptualized as

"a system of constructs and propositions that conjointly demonstrates a logical and yet systematic and coherent account of a phenomenon bounded by some assumptions and conditions" [39].

On the other hand, in terms of its purpose, a theory can also be viewed as a

"coherent set of general propositions used as principles of explanation, understanding and/or prediction of the apparent relationships of certain observed phenomena" [32]. A theory has been empirically tested and verified and can be shown as a schematic diagram, mathematical equation and words.

In its essence, a theory presents a way of studying concepts or variables concerning a phenomenon in order to find or investigate the solution for a research problem. A theory also explains or predicts occurrences by outlining the relationships between concepts or variables which underpin a phenomenon. However, to offer explanations or predictions, theories tend to possess certain characteristics. These characteristics, espoused by academics [40] [41], include:

- Theory is not data, facts, typologies, taxonomies or empirical findings. Theories are not an ad hoc collection of constructs without relationships; they must have propositions (relationships), explanations, and boundary conditions.
- The explanations offered by theories are nomothetic. Thus, they tend to go beyond explaining single events to offer explanations which are generalizable across situations, events, or people. As such, they are less precise, less complete and tend to focus on patterns of events, behavior or phenomena.
- Theories operate at a conceptual level and stem from logic; however, data and findings operate at the empirical or observational level.

Richard Boateng

For a theory to be well understood, there are some foundational premises that need to be set. These are constructs, propositions, logic, and boundary conditions or assumptions [40]. The constructs of a theory define what the theory is about and also explain what concepts are important for understanding a phenomenon. Propositions, on the other hand, are about how these concepts are related to each other. The logic of a theory explains why the concepts are related and the boundary conditions or assumptions probe the "who, when, and where" by bringing out the circumstances under which these concepts and relationships work.

Purpose or Goal of Theory

Gregor has identified four primary goals of a theory which can, arguably, be used as a taxonomy for classifying theories [41]. These goals of a theory are briefly outlined as follows:

- **Analysis and description.** The theory provides a description of the phenomenon of interest, analysis of relationships among those constructs, the degree of generalizability in the constructs and relationships, and the boundaries within which relationships and observations hold.
- **Explanation**. The theory provides an explanation of how, why and when things happen, relying on varying views of causality and methods for argumentation. This explanation will usually be intended to promote greater understanding or insights by others into the phenomenon of interest.
- **Prediction**. The theory states what will happen in the future if certain preconditions hold. The degree of certainty in the prediction is expected to be only approximate or probabilistic in research.
- **Prescription**. A special case of prediction exists where the theory provides a description of the method or structure or both for the construction of an artifact (akin to a recipe). The provision of the recipe implies that the recipe, if acted upon, will cause an artifact of a certain type to come into being.

Apart from informing research and practice, theories also offer many benefits [40]. First, theories provide the underlying logic of the occurrence of a natural or social phenomenon by explaining what the key drivers are and key outcomes of the target phenomenon and why, and what underlying processes are responsible for driving that phenomenon. Second, they aid in sense-making by helping us synthesize prior empirical findings within a theoretical framework and to reconcile contradictory findings by discovering contingent factors influencing the relationship between two constructs in different studies. Third, theories provide guidance for future research by helping identify constructs and relationships that are worthy of further research. Fourth, theories can contribute to cumulative knowledge building by bridging gaps between other theories, and by causing existing theories to be reevaluated in a new light.

However, theories can also have their own share of limitations. As simplified explanations of reality, theories may not always provide adequate explanation of the phenomenon of interest, based on a limited set of constructs and relationships. Theories are designed to be simplified and parsimonious explanations, while the reality may be significantly more complex. Furthermore, theories may impose blinders or limit researchers' "range of vision," causing them to miss out on important concepts that are not defined by the theory [40].

Components of a Theory

Constructs

To explain a phenomenon there is the need for a concept or construct. Constructs are **abstract concepts that explain the phenomenon of interest**. They bring out the generalizable properties related to objects, people or events under study. Some constructs consist of a single concept such as age or weight; and others are multi-dimensional, consisting of multiple underlying concepts, such as performance and motivation.

Despite this distinction all constructs must have a clearly spelt out operational definition to specify how the construct will be measured and at what level of analysis it will be applied (individual, group, organizational, industry, national, regional and global). A construct operates at the theoretical level; hence, a variable is used to measure it at the empirical level. For example, job performance, as an abstract concept, can be expressed as variable in the form of work samples, absenteeism, and/or production count.

A variable is therefore **a characteristic or attribute of an event or phenomenon under study, that can be measured or observed and that varies among the phenomenon being studied** [42]. It is important for a researcher to understand the differences between operating at the theoretical level and that of the empirical level. At the theoretical level, the researcher is concerned with developing abstract concepts about a phenomenon and what relationships exist between those concepts. This is where theories are built. At the empirical level testing the theoretical concepts and relationships is what is important and this is done to see how well they match with observations of reality. This is to ensure the building of better and more robust theories [40].

The constructs are conceived at the theoretical level, while variables are put into use and measured at the empirical (observational) level. The variables at the empirical level are classified as independent, dependent, mediating, or moderating. The independent variables indicate the inputs or causes in the event or phenomenon under investigation, or they are tested to see if they are the cause. The dependent variable on the other hand represents the output or effect. The dependent variable is tested to see if it is the effect of the independent variable. However, variables that explain a relation or provide a causal link between other variables are known as intervening or mediating variables. For example, medical care is one of the intervening variables between income and longevity. People with high incomes tend to have better medical care than those with low incomes. Moderating variables influence or moderate the relationship between two variables and thus produce an interaction effect. A moderator may increase the strength of a relationship, decrease the strength of a relationship, or change the direction of a relationship. For example, age is a moderator of the effect of advertising on food preferences if advertising influences food preference in younger children but not in older children [43].

PROPOSITION

The second building block of a theory is a proposition. Propositions are the relationships between constructs based on some logic [40]. Usually they are stated in a form that is declarative in nature and indicate a cause-effect relationship. Propositions are stated at the theoretical level in a similar way as constructs. Since propositions denote relationships between constructs, they can best be tested by probing the measurable variables of the constructs of a particular phenomenon. When the proposition is stated empirically by indicating the relationship between the variables or constructs, then we have what is called a hypothesis. The difference between a proposition and a hypothesis is seen at the stage or level of formulation or testing. Propositions are formulated at the theoretical level whilst hypotheses are tested at the empirical level.

LOGIC

When propositions are stated there must be a basis for their justification. To justify the proposition of a theory, logic is needed. This is the third building block of a theory. It acts as the binding force that binds the theoretical constructs together and provides a meaning to the relationships between the constructs. Logic provides the explanations that are the bottom lines of any theory. Without it the propositions are meaningless.

ASSUMPTIONS

Finally, theories are limited by assumptions. The assumptions control where the theory can be used and where it be cannot used. For a theory to be properly applied or tested, all of its inherent assumptions that form the boundaries of that theory must be properly understood [40]. Based on the discussions above, what constitutes a theory can be summed up as an interrelated set of constructs or variables which are formed into propositions, or hypotheses, to specify the relationship among variables [42].

Other authors like, Gregor [41], have also proposed similar taxonomies for explaining the components of theory. Gregor discusses that there are:

- **four components,** common to all theories, namely: **means of representation, constructs, statements of relationship** and **scope**; and
- **three components,** contingent on theory purpose, **causal explanations, testable propositions (hypotheses)** and **Prescriptive statements.** Gregor's components of a theory are briefly explained in Exhibit 26.

EXHIBIT 26 GREGOR'S COMPONENTS OF A THEORY

Theory Component (Components Common to All Theory)	Definition
Means of representation	The theory must be represented physically in some way: in words, mathematical
Constructs	These refer to the phenomena of interest in the theory. All of the primary constructs in the theory should be well defined. Many different types of constructs are possible: For example, observational (real) terms, theoretical (nominal) terms and collective terms.
Statements of relationship	These show relationships among the constructs. Again, these may be of many types: associative, compositional, unidirectional, bidirectional, conditional, or causal. The nature of the relationship specified depends on the purpose of the theory. Very simple relationships can be specified: For example, "x is a member of class A."
Scope	The scope is specified by the degree of generality of the statements of relationships (signified by modal qualifiers such as "some," "many," "all," and "never") and statements of boundaries showing the limits of generalizations.
Theory Component (Components Contingent on Theory Purpose)	Definition
Causal explanations	The theory gives statements of relationships among phenomena that show causal reasoning (not covering law or probabilistic reasoning alone).
Testable propositions (hypotheses)	Statements of relationships between constructs are stated in such a form that they can be tested empirically.
Prescriptive statements	Statements in the theory specify how people can accomplish something in practice (e.g., construct an artifact or develop a strategy).

Source: [41]

Attributes of a Good Theory

Researchers have proposed a number of characteristics or attributes of a good theory. In this section we will outline a summary of these attributes compiled by the authors, Bhattacherjee [40], Gregor [41] and Creswell [42]. The attributes are:

(1) **Logical consistency**: this involves ensuring that the building blocks of a theory (constructs, propositions, boundary conditions, and assumptions) are logically coherent in their relationship with each other. To test whether a theory is a good one or not, the elements of the theory should not contradict each other [40].

(2) **Explanatory power**: when there is a theory about a phenomenon, the theory should be capable of explaining the phenomenon so well that no other existing theory can do it better. This means that theories must possess the overall power of explaining or predicting the behavior of the phenomenon. It is only through this that the theory can be said to be good [40].

(3) **Falsifiability**: there should be inherent possibility to refute a theory or prove it to be false. Basically, falsifiability is **the belief that for any theory to have credence, it must be inherently disprovable before it can become accepted as a theory.** Theories are potentially disprovable if empirical data which has been found by researchers does not match with the theoretical constructs or propositions of the theory. There is a distinction between a theory that is falsifiable and that which should be falsified. The two are not the same. The falsifiability of a theory should be based on empirical evidence. When a theory is falsified on this basis, then there is clear evidence to suggest that the theory is not a good one. Bhattacherjee gives an example that, sometimes theories are falsified by their theoretical propositions: "Tautological statements, such as "a day with high temperatures is a hot day", are not empirically testable because a hot day is defined (and measured) as a day with high temperatures, and hence, such statements cannot be viewed as a theoretical proposition" [40]. Thus, what makes a theory a theory is its ability to be tested or examined by empirical data.

(4) **Parsimony**: theories are meant to be very simplified and generalizable explanations of phenomena. This means that if there is a complex phenomenon

out there and there is a theory about the phenomenon, the theory must explain the phenomenon and its complexities in a very simple form. The parsimony of a theory is about **how simple the theory is and how it can be generalized to other contexts, settings and phenomena** [40]. For example, the technology acceptance model [44]posits that two particular beliefs on the part of users, perceived usefulness and perceived ease-of-use, are of primary relevance for technology acceptance behaviors. The theory espouses that the acceptance level of any technology is fundamentally affected by the user's perception of ease of use and usefulness. This theory leads to testable propositions that can be investigated empirically. The simplicity of the theory makes it applicable to testing the acceptance behavior for a diversity of technologies.

Classification of Theory

Theories can be classified by a number of taxonomies, including the goal and components, degree of theorization, the disciplinary domains, the level of analysis and time. This section of the chapter will discuss the five taxonomies outlined.

TYPES OF THEORY BY GOAL/PURPOSE

The goals of theory, as discussed earlier, can be combined to formulate five types of theory [41], outlined below (see [35] for examples):

(1) **Analysis** - says what is.
  - The theory does not extend beyond analysis and description. No causal relationships among phenomena are specified and no predictions are made.
(2) **Explanation** - says what is, how, why, when, and where.
  - The theory provides explanations but does not aim to predict with any precision. There are no testable propositions.
(3) **Prediction** - says what is and what will be.
  - The theory provides predictions and has testable propositions but does not have well-developed justificatory causal explanations.
(4) **Explanation and Prediction (EP)** - says what is, how, why, when, where, and what will be.
  - Theory provides predictions and has both testable propositions and causal explanations.
(5) **Design and Action** - says how to do something.
  - The theory gives explicit prescriptions (e.g., methods, techniques, principles of form and function) for constructing an artifact.

DEGREE OF THEORIZATION

This classification was previously discussed in Chapter 2. A theory, as earlier defined, is a "coherent set of general propositions used as principles of explanation, understanding and/or prediction of the apparent relationships of certain **observed** phenomena" [32]. Theories have been empirically tested and have gained some degree of acceptance to explain phenomena by the scientific community in a particular research discipline. Conceptual frameworks or approaches, on the other hand, are analytical schemes which simplify reality to make it easier to discuss, analyze or research. They simplify reality by selecting certain phenomena/ variables and **suggesting** certain relationships between them [33]. Conceptual approaches are suggestive in nature, and are, arguably, yet to gain sufficient empirical testing to be accepted as theory. Thus, theories and conceptual approaches can be differentiated according to a hierarchy moving from shallower conceptualization to deeper theoretically-based approaches – as follows [35]:

(1) **Theoretically-based approaches** which make clear use of an identifiable theory that can be applied or tested.

(2) **Framework-based approaches** that make use of a framework for analysis that is derived from a body of theoretical work.

(3) **Model-based approaches** that are applied, but without reference to a deeper body of knowledge.

(4) **Concept-based approaches** that make use of a defined concept such as 'information poverty', but which is not theoretically grounded.

(5) **Category based approaches** that make use of a prescribed set of factors to carry out analysis.

LEVEL OF ANALYSIS

Theories can be classified according to the level of application or analysis. As such they can be:

(1) **Micro-level Theory: Seeks to analyze, explain or predict actions and interactions at the individual level**. However, it may also take the local context in which the actions and interactions occur into consideration. For example, the technology acceptance model tends to explain technology acceptance at the individual level.

(2) **Meso-level Theory: Seeks to analyze, explain or predict actions and interactions at the meso-level**. These may include theories of organizations, social movements and communities. For example, the Resource-Based Theory of the Firm explains how firms compete based on their resources.

Other theories may go beyond one firm to examine a collection of firms or an industry.

(3) **Macro-Level Theory: Seeks to analyze, explain or predict actions and interactions at the macro-level**. These theories explain larger aggregates such as social institutions and cultural societies, and whole societies. Examples are the Modernization Theory in development studies and Hofstede's Cultural Dimensions in Management.

Other authors attest to these classifications using different or comparable taxonomies [2]. Reeves *et al.* [45] classify theories as micro-level, mid-range (local systems; recognition of cultural or contextual variations) and grand theory (universal, societal level theories). The importance of these classifications is for researchers to understand and identify the appropriate theories to address research problems within a specific unit of analysis. For example, it may be challenging to use a micro-level theory to analyze actions and interactions at the macro-level.

Disciplinary domains

Researchers tend to develop theories to analyze, explain or predict phenomena in their respective disciplines. Hence, each discipline has theories to study society within the assumptions and beliefs espoused by researchers in that discipline. That said, researchers can also borrow theories from different disciplines to conduct disciplinary, and interdisciplinary or cross-disciplinary research. For example, information systems theories originate from social science and other disciplines. A number of them have been compiled and can be assessed at: http://istheory. byu.edu/.

Theories in Economics and Finance include: the Arbitrage Pricing Theory, Rational Choice Theory, Prospect Theory, Cumulative Prospect Theory, Monte Carlo Option Model, Binomial Options Pricing Model, Gordon Model, International Fisher Effect, Black Model, and Legal Origins Theory. The Arbitrage Pricing Theory, For example, addresses the general theory of asset pricing. Read more at: www.tinyurl.com/ financetheories

In categorizing by themes, economics and finance theories may cover:

Global Trade

- Comparative advantage
- Heckscher-Ohlin trade model
- New trade theory
- Optimal currency area
- The impossible trinity
- Purchasing power parity

Choice

- Rational choice
- Game theory
- Public choice
- Expected utility theory
- Prospect theory

Markets, Tax & Spend Policies

- The invisible hand
- Marginalism
- The tragedy of the commons
- Property rights
- Polluter pays principle
- Adverse selection
- Moral hazard
- Tax incidence
- Excess burden
- Supply-side economics
- Crowding out
- Efficient market hypothesis
- Rent seeking

TIME

Classifying theories by time refers to **how long the theory has been around** – i.e. when was it developed. Thus, some theories may be viewed as mature theories. For example, a theory that was first proposed in some period, like 1960s or 1990s, is likely to have been widely applied and tested in different disciplines, revised to make it applicable to different contexts, and perhaps, used as the basis of new theories. Arguably, the Theory of Reasoned-Action can be considered a mature theory. The very popular Technology Acceptance model (TAM) was formulated by Davis [44] from the Theory of Reasoned Action (TRA) [46] as a concise, complete reliable and valid model for predicting user acceptance. On the other hand, theories that are now gaining acceptance or being tested may be considered as emerging theories. An example is the Process Virtualization Theory which provides constructs to assess the amenability of 'physical' processes to virtual environments [47].

Schematic Representation of Theories and Conceptual Frameworks

Theories and conceptual frameworks can be schematically expressed in a number of ways including [33]:

CAUSE AND EFFECT FRAMEWORKS

Cause and effect conceptual frameworks identify the various factors which affect a phenomenon. They are often the basis of hypotheses type of research. The arrows are converted into series of hypothesis (Exhibit 27).

EXHIBIT 27 EXAMPLE OF A CAUSE AND EFFECT MODEL

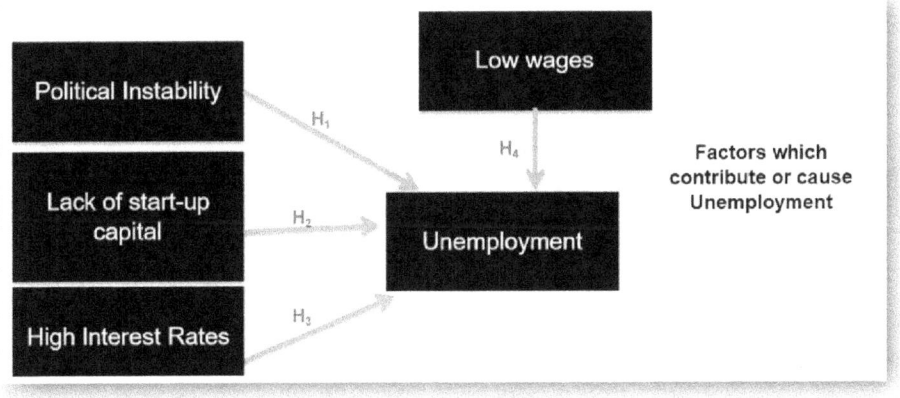

STAGES IN A PROCESS

Process-based conceptual frameworks show how concepts are related in a process, which have stages/phases and lead to an outcome. The sequence can be a linear or cyclical process (Exhibit 28).

EXHIBIT 28 EXAMPLE OF A PROCESS-BASED MODEL

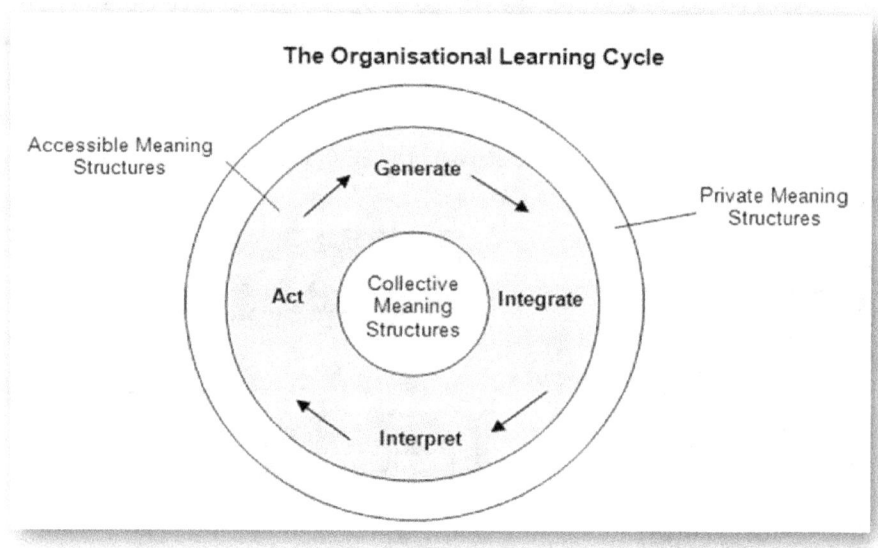

Source: [97]

HIERARCHICAL RELATIONSHIPS

Hierarchy-based conceptual frameworks show how concepts are related in higher or lower positions on a scale. The higher concept or factor has to be at the apex and the lower concept at the base of the hierarchy (Exhibit 34).

EXHIBIT 29 EXAMPLE OF A HIERARCHY-BASED FRAMEWORK

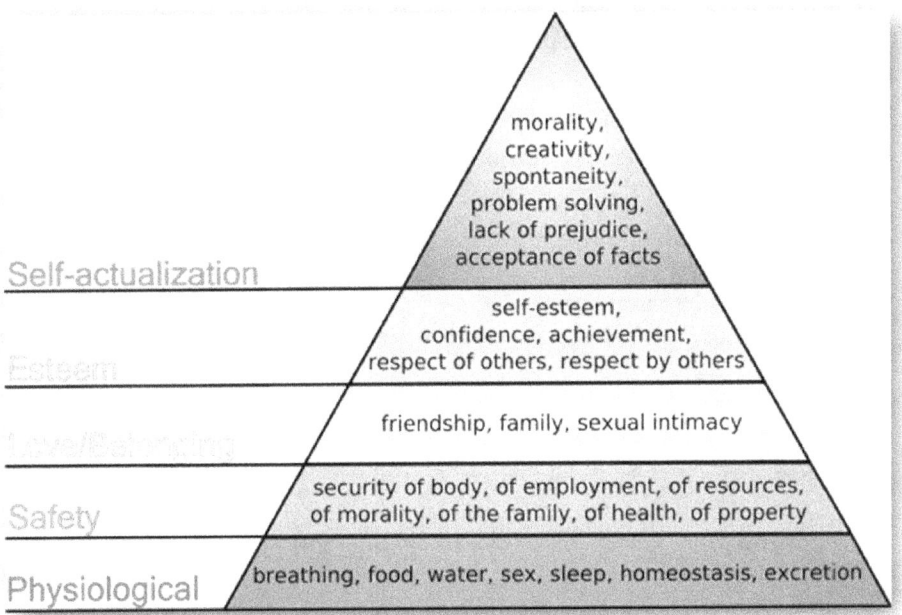

Maslow's Hierarchy of Needs [98]
Picture source: J. Finkelstein-

GAP ANALYSIS

Gap-based conceptual frameworks use concepts to expose gaps in the phenomenon which need to be addressed. Gaps may show a discrepancy or failure in the phenomenon (Exhibit 30).

EXHIBIT 30 EXAMPLE OF A GAP-BASED FRAMEWORK

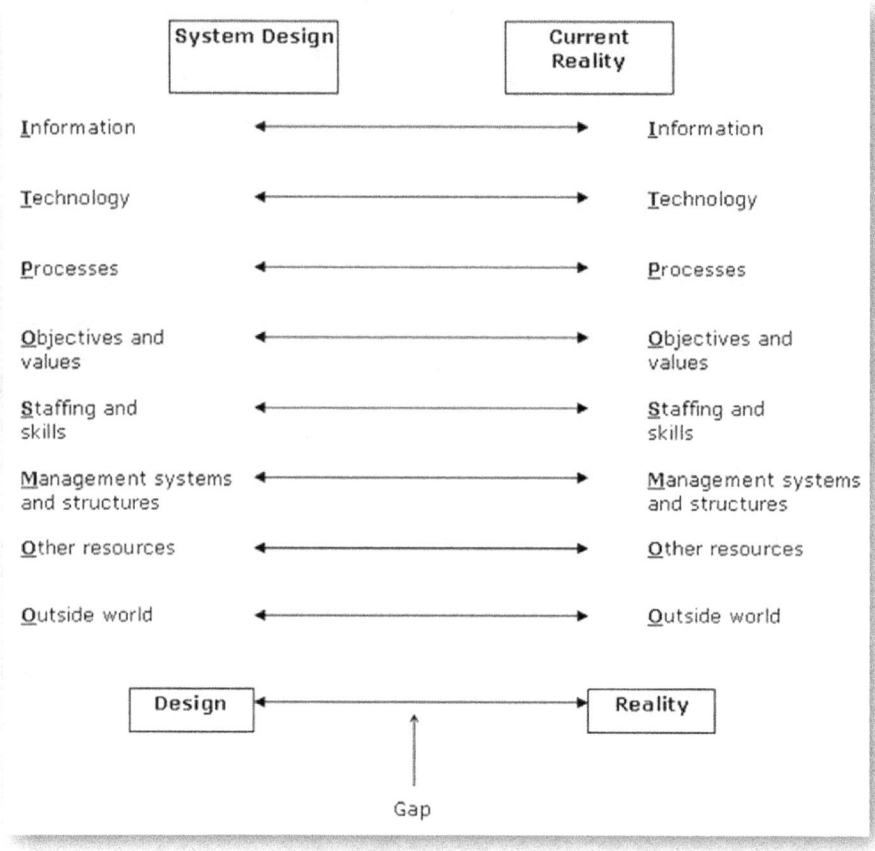

Design Reality Gap (43)

MAPS AND COORDINATES

Map-based conceptual frameworks show how concepts are related through vertical and horizontal scales of a map. The most common map-based conceptual frameworks are two scale maps: in a two-by-two matrix or an axis divided into two (Exhibit 31).

EXHIBIT 31 EXAMPLE OF A MAP-BASED FRAMEWORK

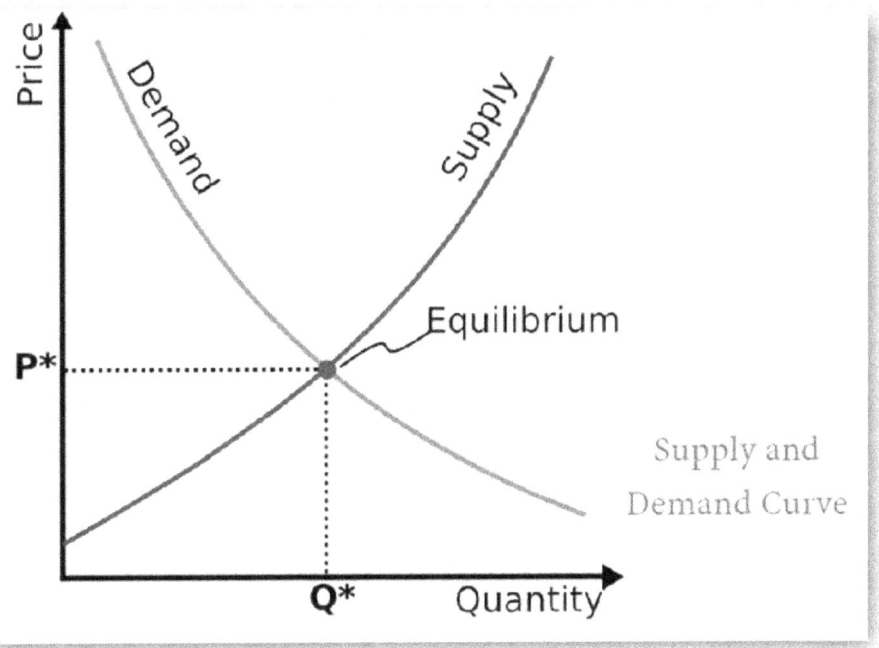

Supply and Demand Curve

FORCE-FIELD DIAGRAM

Force-Field Diagram conceptual frameworks show the duality between concepts. They demonstrate the competing forces which can bring about a change in social phenomena (Exhibit 32).

EXHIBIT 32 EXAMPLE OF A FORCE-FIELD DIAGRAM

Driving Forces	Restraining Forces
Competitive opportunity	Lack of resources
New Employees	Manager attitude
Stakeholder pressure	Low awareness of environment

THEORY AND THE RESEARCH FRAMEWORK: THE LINKAGES

The research framework outlines the processes to study the variables or concepts concerning phenomena under investigation. It is called a research framework because it frames the research. It gives boundaries to the research by indicating what should be part of the research or not. It also helps the researcher to formulate the research questions. Thus, a researcher needs a research framework to steer a research. However, this research framework can be developed purely from theory, and thus, can be called a theoretical framework or it can be developed from a review of literature, concepts and theories to develop a tentative (suggestive) *theory* and thus can be called a conceptual framework.

Research frameworks can, therefore, exist in the form of a theory/theoretical framework or a conceptual framework. The conceptual framework consists of the system of concepts, assumptions, expectations, beliefs, and theories that guide and inform the research [48] [49]. The conceptual framework is a conception or model of what is out there that the research seeks to investigate, and also what is going on with these issues or phenomenon and what is causing it to change in the way that it does. It is therefore a tentative (suggestive) *theory* of the phenomenon that is being investigated. The *theory* is considered 'tentative' at this stage because of its unsettled nature as compared to an existing theory which is already out there and can be drawn upon to inform the research. The 'tentative' theory in the conceptual framework is a provisionary guide that will inform the rest of the research work or design in terms of refining the goals of the research and developing the right research questions.

Another view of the conceptual framework is to see it as something that the researcher *constructs, and* not something that will be found by the researcher in the literature. It means, therefore, that a lot can be borrowed from elsewhere, and with some coherence this framework can be built by the researcher. However, the researcher cannot do this without paying attention to what theories are already out there and how this can inform the development of the conceptual framework.

Finally, the research framework can form part of the literature review or be an outcome of the literature review (see (44)). Other authors also separate the research framework from the literature review (see (24)). Both approaches are welcome; it is a matter of preference, paper submission requirements and the structure of the research paper.

Summary

A theory is an organized, coherent, and systematic articulation of a set of issues that are communicated as a meaningful whole. Theories provide complex and comprehensive conceptual understandings of things that cannot be pinned down: how societies work, how organizations operate, and why people interact in certain ways [45].

In this chapter we explored the relevance of a theory, components of a theory and the classification of theories. It also outlined the schematic representations of theories with examples from existing theories and conceptual frameworks.

In the next chapter we will discuss research methodology.

Chapter Discussions

QUESTION 1
What do you understand by the term theory and why is it important in information systems research? Use examples to explain the constructs and assumptions of a theory.

QUESTION 2
Discuss the tenets of the Technology Acceptance Model (TAM) and explain the motivations underpinning its subsequent revisions into TAM 2 and TAM 3. Do you think there is a possibility for TAM 4?

QUESTION 3
Briefly explain one theory or conceptual model you know that can be applied to carry out research or even conduct an analysis of an industry or firm.

CHAPTER 6

Research Methodology

Objectives

This chapter explains qualitative research methods; describes the types of qualitative research methods; and differentiates between quantitative and qualitative methods.

Qualitative and Quantitative Research Explained

TO BEGIN LET us revisit our previous discussion on research methods. Qualitative research (QR) **tends to explore the meanings, attitudes, values, and beliefs people associate with a phenomenon in order to establish a better understanding, rather than to test to either support or disprove a relationship**. Qualitative research focuses on the interpretation of phenomena in their natural settings to make sense in terms of the meanings people bring to these settings [50]. Patton considers QR as "an effort to understand situations in their uniqueness as part of a particular context and the interactions there" [51]. This approach is useful for describing the nature of a problem, issue, situation or phenomenon. QR is arguably unstructured as it starts with general research problems and not by formulating hypotheses (hypotheses may emerge from the data analysis). It uses relatively unstructured instruments (e.g. interviews, observations, etcetera) and "intense" data collection (e.g. over extended periods of time). Data is collected from a small, purposive sample (not random) which may or may not be representative of the larger population. The results are presented mainly or exclusively in words. It is more about explanation, and de-emphasizing generalizations to the population. Throughout this process, the researcher is aware of his/her own orientations, biases or experiences and personal interaction with subjects or the context of the study. The qualitative approach allows flexibility in all activities of the research process.

Quantitative research **seeks to determine the extent of a problem or the existence of a relationship between aspects of a phenomenon by quantifying the variation**. Quantitative research often seeks to test to support or disprove a proposed relationship between two or more aspects of a phenomenon. Quantitative research is structured because it starts with specific hypotheses or questions derived from theory/previous research, and uses objective instruments (e.g. fixed choice questionnaires, attitude scales, et cetera) to collect data from a selected sample. The results are presented using statistics and inferences made to the population. Throughout this process, the researcher is viewed as being independent from subjects involved in the research. Hence, there is a "distance" between researcher and subjects, and an emphasis on following the research design.

The differences between qualitative and quantitative research are briefly summarized by Mack *et al.* [52], outlined in Exhibit 33.

EXHIBIT 33 COMPARISON OF QUANTITATIVE AND QUALITATIVE RESEARCH APPROACHES

	Qualitative	Quantitative
General framework	Seek to explore phenomena	Seek to confirm hypotheses about phenomena
	Instruments use more flexible, iterative style of eliciting and categorizing responses to questions	Instruments use more rigid style of eliciting and categorizing responses to questions
	Use semi-structured methods such as in-depth interviews, focus groups, and participant observation	Use highly structured methods such as questionnaires, surveys, and structured observation
Analytical objectives	To describe variation	To quantify variation
	To describe and explain relationships	To predict causal relationships
	To describe individual experiences	To describe characteristics of a population
	To describe group norms	
Question format	Open-ended	Closed-ended
Data format	Textual (obtained from audiotapes, videotapes, and field notes)	Numerical (obtained by assigning numerical values to responses)
Flexibility in study design	Some aspects of the study are flexible (For example, the addition, exclusion, or wording of interview questions)	Study design is stable from beginning to end
	Participant responses affect how and which questions researchers ask next	Participant responses do not influence or determine how and which questions researchers ask next
	Study design is iterative, that is, data collection and research questions are adjusted according to what is learned	Study design is subject to statistical assumptions and conditions

Source: [52]

Key Features of Qualitative Research

A number of features of qualitative research have been espoused in literature. Flick [53] identified four features of QR, namely:

1. Appropriateness of methods and theories;
2. Perspectives of the participants and their diversity;
3. Reflexivity of the researcher and the research; and
4. Variety of approaches and methods in qualitative research.

Largely agreeing with Flick, Creswell [54] proposed eight features of QR, namely:

1. Natural setting;
2. Researcher key instrument;
3. Multiple methods;
4. Complex reasoning through inductive and deductive logic;
5. Participants' meanings;
6. Emergent design;
7. Reflexivity; and
8. Holistic account.

A more comprehensive set of twelve features has been documented by Patton [51]. The twelve features are categorized in three key strategies: Design Strategies; Data-Collection and Fieldwork Strategies; and Analysis Strategies. The features are briefly described below.

Design Strategies

1. **Naturalistic inquiry** – QR aims to study real-world situations as they unfold naturally; it is nonmanipulative and noncontrolling. QR is open to whatever emerges (lack of predetermined constraints on findings).
2. **Emergent design flexibility** – QR is open to adapting inquiry as understanding deepens and/or situations change; the QR researcher avoids getting

locked into rigid designs that eliminate responsiveness and pursues new paths of discovery as they emerge.

3. **Purposeful sampling** – Respondents in samples or units of analysis are purposively selected because they are "information rich" and illuminative, that is, they offer useful manifestations of the phenomenon of interest.

DATA-COLLECTION AND FIELDWORK STRATEGIES

4. **Qualitative Data** – Primary forms of data are observations, interviews and documents. QR embraces observations that yield detailed, thick description; inquiry in depth; interviews that capture direct quotations about people's personal perspectives and experiences; and careful document review.

5. **Personal experience and engagement** – The QR researcher has direct contact with and gets close to the people, situation, and phenomenon under study; the QR researcher's personal experiences and insights are an important part of the inquiry and critical to understanding the phenomenon.

6. **Empathic neutrality and mindfulness** – The QR researcher should have an empathic stance in interviewing – one which seeks vicarious understanding without judgment (neutrality) by showing openness, sensitivity, respect, awareness, and responsiveness; in observation it means being fully present (mindfulness).

7. **Dynamic systems** – The QR researcher needs to be attentive to process; assume change as ongoing whether the focus is on an individual, an organization, a community, or an entire culture; therefore, being mindful of and attentive to system and situation dynamics and interactions between components of a phenomenon.

ANALYSIS STRATEGIES

8. **Unique case orientation** - The QR researcher needs to assume that each case is special and unique; the first level of analysis is being true to, respecting, and capturing the details of the individual cases being studied. Cross-case analysis follows from and depends on the quality of individual case studies.

9. **Inductive analysis and creative synthesis** - The QR researcher needs to be immersed in the details and specifics of the data to discover important patterns, themes, and interrelationships; it begins by exploring, then confirming, guided by analytical principles rather than rules, and ends with a creative synthesis.

10. **Holistic perspective** - The whole phenomenon under study is understood as a complex system that is more than the sum of its parts; focuses on complex interdependencies and system dynamics that cannot meaningfully be reduced to a few discrete variables and linear, cause effect relationships. The question to be answered is, how does what I observe inform or explain the whole...what matters?

11. **Context sensitivity** – QR places findings in a social, historical, and temporal context; careful about, even dubious of, the possibility or meaningfulness of generalizations across time and space;

12. **Voice, perspective, and reflexivity** – The researcher owns and is reflective about his or her own voice and perspective; a credible voice conveys authenticity and trustworthiness; complete objectivity being impossible and pure subjectivity undermining credibility, the researcher's focus becomes balance; understanding and depicting the world authentically in all its complexity while being self-analytical, politically aware, and reflexive in consciousness.

Types of Qualitative Research

Qualitative research primarily draws on nonnumeric data. But to generate this qualitative data, QR researchers have to use a qualitative research method. In this section, we will discuss four types of qualitative research [55]: Phenomenology; Ethnography; Grounded theory; and Case study.

Johnson and Christensen's excellent summary of the key characteristics (i.e., purpose, origin, data-collection methods, data analysis, and report focus) of the four types of qualitative research is outlined in Exhibit 34.

EXHIBIT 34 CHARACTERISTICS OF FOUR TYPES OF QUALITATIVE RESEARCH

	Phenomenology	Ethnography	Case Study	Grounded Theory
Research Purpose	To describe one or more individuals' experiences of a phenomenon (e.g., the experience of the death of a loved one)	To describe the cultural characteristics of a group of people and to describe cultural scenes	To describe one or more cases in-depth and address the research questions and issues.	To inductively generate a grounded theory describing and explaining a phenomenon
Disciplinary origin	Philosophy	Anthropology	Multidisciplinary roots, including business, law, social sciences, medicine, and education	Sociology
Primary data collection method	In-depth interviews with up to 10–15 people	Participant observation over an extended period of time (e.g., one month to a year). Interviews with informants	Multiple methods are used (e.g., interviews, observations, documents)	Interviews with 20–30 people. Observations are also frequently used
Data analysis approach	List significant statements, determine meaning of statements, and identify the essence of the phenomenon	Holistic description and search for cultural themes in data.	Holistic description and search for themes shedding light on the case. May also include cross-case analysis	Begin with open coding, then axial coding, and end with selective coding
Narrative report focus	Rich description of the essential or invariant structures (i.e., the common characteristics, or essences) of the experience	Rich description of context and cultural themes	Rich description of the context and operation of the case or cases. Discussion of themes, issues, and implications	Description of topic and people being studied. End with a presentation of the grounded theory. May also list propositions

Source: [55]

PHENOMENOLOGY

Phenomenology describes the meaning of one or several individuals of their lived experiences of a concept or a phenomenon. Phenomenologists seek to answer the question, *what are the meaning, structure, and essence of the lived experiences of this phenomenon by an individual or by many individuals* [55]? Phenomenologists search for the invariant structures of individual's experiences or to put it in other words, 'the essences of their experience'. For example, what is the essence of PhD students' experiences in the University of Ghana Business School? The basic objective is to develop a description of the universal essence. As such, phenomenologists focus on describing what all participants have in common as they experience a phenomenon.

Creswell [42] identified two approaches to phenomenology as:

- **Hermeneutic phenomenology**[5] - a descriptive and interpretive research which focuses on lived experience (phenomenology) and interpreting the "texts" of life (hermeneutics).
- **Empirical, transcendental, or psychological phenomenology** - requires the researcher to 'bracket' or temporarily put aside personal attitudes and beliefs concerning a phenomenon before engaging the research respondents through interviews. Bracketing personal attitudes and beliefs heightens the consciousness of the researcher thereby allowing the researcher to see and examine the phenomenon from the perspective of those who experienced it.

In both approaches the researcher will need to delve into what has been experienced in terms of the phenomenon and the contexts or situations which influenced or affected experiences of the phenomenon. They tend to use in-depth interviews as the common method for uncovering the life-worlds of individuals. The data collected is clustered into themes and examined from multiple perspectives (mediating between different meanings of lived experiences) to develop a rich description of the essential or invariant structures (i.e., the common characteristics, or essences) of the experience.

> **Example** [56]: Eight clinical psychology practicum-level trainees were interviewed to obtain their experiences of good supervision. Meaning units were identified from these and a meaning structure was identified and refined into the essence or essential elements of good supervisory experiences shared by a majority in this context. Source: [57]

ETHNOGRAPHY

Ethnography is a qualitative research method which involves a description of people and nature of a phenomenon. An ethnographic description includes the cultural

---

5 "Phenomenology is usually described as studying the essence, and hermeneutics as studying the processes of interpretation. There is a link between hermeneutics and phenomenology, but it is very complicated and there are unsurpassable differences" [100].

characteristics of a group of people and their cultural scenes. Ethnography involves exploring the nature of phenomena and working with unstructured data, as well as analyzing data through interpretation of the meanings attributed by research respondents. This method involves primary observations and interviews with informants conducted by a researcher over an extended period of time.

Since the origins of ethnography is in anthropology, the researcher needs to have some grounding in the discipline to effectively use this QR method. The time to collect data is extensive, involving prolonged time in the field. The immersion of the researcher into the culture is also necessary to paint a picture of the culture (the beliefs, traditions, practices and behaviors) that is thorough, accurate, and vivid. However, the constraints of time and resources from the data collection may deter researchers from this QR method.

> **Example** [56]: Native American students training to be teachers were followed through interviews over a five year period to chart the progress towards a goal of facilitating the development of Native American teachers and to better understand and address their unique problems. Their beliefs, views about self, and concerns were presented.
>
> Source: [58]

GROUNDED THEORY

The method derives its name from 'a theory that is "grounded" in the data'. Being grounded in data means the theory is localized, dealing with a specific situation like how women micro-entrepreneurs handle multiple responsibilities [56]. The primary question being answered is *What theory or explanation emerges from an analysis of the data collected about this phenomenon* [42]? The method requires the researcher to compare collected units of data against one another until categories, properties, and tentative hypotheses (propositions) that state the relations between these categories and properties emerge. Data is therefore analyzed to unravel elements of experience and to determine interrelationships which build a theory that enables the researcher to understand a phenomenon. Other researchers describe the process as the development of inductive, "bottom-up," theory that is "grounded" directly in the empirical data.

To analyze data:

(1) The researcher begins with **open coding**, reading data transcripts line-by-line and identifying and coding the concepts/major categories found in the data [55].

(2) The next stage is **axial coding**, organizing concepts to make them more abstract. To do this, the researcher identifies one open coding concept to focus on (called the "core" phenomenon), and then goes back to the data and creates other related concepts around this core phenomenon [55]. In the process of organization, the researcher identifies key factors related to the core phenomenon:

   - **Causal conditions:** factors which caused the core phenomenon.
   - **Contextual/Intervening conditions:** broad and specific situational factors that influence the strategies and consequences (outcomes from using the strategies).

(3) The final step, then, is **selective coding**, in which the researcher develops propositions from the key concepts, and finalizes the grounded theory. The theory developed should have four important characteristics:

   - Fit (i.e., Does the theory correspond to real-world data?),
   - Understanding (i.e., Is the theory clear and understandable?),
   - Generality (i.e., Is the theory abstract enough to move beyond the specifics in the original research study?),
   - Control (i.e., Can the theory be applied to produce real-world results?).

It is important to note that the data collection and analysis continues throughout the study [55]. Further, the researcher needs to understand the relevance of theoretical sensitivity and theoretical saturation. Theoretical sensitivity is about being sensitive to what data is important in developing the grounded theory. Theoretical saturation occurs when no new concepts are emerging from the data and the theory is well validated. At this stage, it can be concluded that the grounded theory process is "complete" [56].

The primary outcome of this study is a theory with specific components: a core phenomenon, causal conditions, strategies, conditions and context, and consequences.

The researcher faces the difficulty of determining when concepts are saturated or when the theory is sufficiently detailed [42].

Example [56]: Student perceptions of the residential environment educational program from a school were collected from 2779 students at 31 schools. A grounded theory approach was used to discover which areas were most interesting, most confusing, and most meaningful. Source: [59]

CASE STUDY

A case is a bounded system (e.g., a person, a group, an activity, a process) [56]. A case study represents a descriptive intensive analysis of the bounded system. The bounded system becomes the unit of analysis for the case. According to Yin [60], three conditions aid in the selection of a method for research; the type of research question posed, the extent of control over actual behavioral events and the degree of focus on contemporary as opposed to historical events. These influence the choice of; experiments, surveys, archival analysis histories and case studies as a research method. Particularly, Yin [60] proposes case study, when a "how" or "why" question is being asked about a contemporary set of events over which the investigator has little or no control. Case study also facilitates the contribution of knowledge in an area which is characterized by a rapid pace of change in the nature and complexities of artifacts and issues involved [61]. Yin (1994) outlined four applications of case study research:

- To explain complex causal links in real-life interventions;
- To describe the real-life context in which the intervention has occurred;
- To describe the intervention itself; and
- To explore those situations in which the intervention being evaluated has no clear set of outcomes.

Other researchers concurring with Yin also argue that case study enables the spotlight or microscopic evaluation of these selected social factors or processes within real-life contexts or natural settings so as to provide a strong test of prevailing explanations (theoretical propositions) or ideas and to refine knowledge [62]. As the phenomenon being studied is not always distinguishable from its context, case study comprises an all-encompassing method which incorporates specific techniques to guide data collection and analysis in direct relation to clearly stated theoretical assumptions [62] [60].

Types of Case Study
Researchers have also proposed several classifications of case study research. Two different classifications, from two authors, Yin and Stake, will be discussed in this

chapter. Yin [60] classifies case studies into three types: Exploratory - explore an area where little is known or little research has been done; Explanatory case studies – appropriate for doing causal investigations; and Descriptive - requires a theory to guide data collection – the theory should be clearly stated in advance and be reviewed to form the basis of the design of the descriptive case study. Stake also classifies case study research into three types: Intrinsic - when the researcher has an interest in understanding the particulars of the case; Instrumental - when the case is used to understand more than what is obvious to the observer; Collective - when a group of cases is studied and compared in a single research study [63].

In all of the above types of case studies, there can be single-case or multiple-case applications. Multiple case studies stem from studying multiple bounded systems. Multiple case studies offer the advantages of aiding research focused on theory building or explanation, and replication – either literal or theoretical replication [60]. These replication techniques can aid in the development of a rich, theoretical framework and make the explanation of the phenomena being studied relatively more compelling and more robust. However, a careful consideration is necessary since multiple case studies may require extensive resources and time that could be beyond the means of a single independent researcher [63].

Designing Case Study
A number of steps for case study design have been proposed by researchers. Yin [60] outlined the following steps:

1. Design the case study protocol:
   - determine the required skills; develop and review the protocol
2. Conduct the case study:
   - prepare for data collection; distribute questionnaire; conduct interviews
3. Analyze case study evidence:
   - determine analytic strategy
4. Develop conclusions, recommendations, and implications based on the evidence.

A more comprehensive outline which can also be adopted entails the following steps:

1. Identify research question
    *   The researcher has to define the "case" to be studied. The case serves as the unit of analysis, hence should be reflected in the research question.
2. Determine types of case study
    *   The researcher can select between single and multiple case studies. The researcher can also choose to keep the case holistic or to have embedded subcases within an overall holistic case.
3. Select participants or groups
    *   The researcher needs to define the boundary for data sources. Boundary refers to how the case might be constrained in terms of time, events, and processes. This may be challenging. Some case studies may not have clean beginning and ending points, and the researcher will need to set boundaries that adequately surround the case.
4. Collect data
    *   Case studies are developed through detailed, in-depth data collection involving multiple sources of information (e.g., observations, interviews, audiovisual material, and documents and reports).
    *   Case study is known as a triangulated research strategy. Triangulation is the use of more than one approach to address a research question in order to enhance confidence, ensure accuracy and embrace alternative explanations. Denzin [64] identified four types of triangulation: Data source triangulation, when the researcher looks for the data to remain the same in different contexts; Investigator triangulation, when several investigators examine the same phenomenon; Theory triangulation, when investigators with different viewpoints interpret the same results; and Methodological triangulation, when one approach is followed by another, to increase confidence in the interpretation.
5. Analyze data
    *   To be discussed in the next Chapter.

6. Compose the report
   - The reports have to be rich (i.e., vivid and detailed) and holistic (i.e., describes the whole and its parts) description of the case and its context.
7. Evaluate the validity and reliability
   - To be discussed in the next Chapter.

CRITICISMS OF CASE STUDIES

Case study research has also been subject to criticism on the grounds of non-representativeness and a lack of rigor and statistical generalizability [65] [60]. Walsham [66] emphasizes that the validity of case study is based on the "plausibility and cogency of the logical reasoning applied in describing and presenting the results from the cases and in drawing conclusions from them". Yin [60] further defends that case studies are used for analytical generalizations where the researcher's aim is to generalize a particular set of results to some broader theoretical propositions and not to enumerate frequencies (statistical generalization). The objective is to move from statistical generalization towards theoretical generalization, where one asks, "what does this case tell us about a specific theory (or theoretical proposition)?" [63]. Case studies are fundamentally theoretical, designed to develop, refine and test theories through the logic of replication – either predicting similar results (literal replication) or producing contrasting results for predictable reasons (theoretical replication) [60] [63]. Moreover, the "goal of understanding a phenomenon from the point of view of the participants and their particular social and institutional context is largely lost, when textual data are quantified" [67].

FORMS OF QUALITATIVE DATA[6]

Researchers tend to fairly agree on the forms of qualitative data. According to Patton [51] qualitative findings [research] grow out of three kinds of data collection: (1) **in-depth; open-ended interviews**; (2) **direct observation**; and (3) **written documents**. Creswell tends to agree with these three forms of data but also includes a fourth one: (1) **interviews;** (2) **observation**; (3) **documents and (4) Audio-visual** (audio, pictures, mobile phone text, social media, video etcetera) [42]. Yin [60]identified six primary sources of evidence for case study research, namely: (1) **documentation**; (2) **archival**

---

6 Questionnaire design is briefly discussed in Appendix A

records; (3) **interviews**; (4) **direct observation**; (5) **participant observation**; and (6) **physical artifacts**.

These forms of qualitative data are briefly discussed below [68] [69]:

- **Documents** could be in the form of material in textual format including company/industry reports, media accounts, letters, memoranda, agendas, and national statistics/reports. Documents may be private (restricted access and perhaps internal to the firm under study) and may be public (available for public access). Some documents may have to be purchased in order to have access; an example is a report which is only accessible in print. The validity of the documents should be carefully reviewed (checking source, currency and relevance) so as to avoid the collection of incorrect or irrelevant data. Documents enable researchers to corroborate evidence gathered from other sources. However, overreliance on documents as evident in case study design should be avoided; data should be triangulated from as many sources as possible.
- **Archival records** are relevant in research which requires maps, service records, charts, lists of names, survey data, and even personal records such as diaries. However, the validity of the archival records should be carefully reviewed (checking source, currency and relevance) so as to avoid the collection of incorrect or irrelevant data.
- **Observation**

  Direct Observation in a qualitative research occurs when the investigator makes a site visit to gather data. The observations could be formal or casual activities, but the reliability of the observation is the main concern. Using multiple observers is one way to guard against this problem. Observer effect can also occur when subjects tend to behave differently in the presence of an observer.

  Participant Observation is a unique mode of observation in which the researcher may actually participate in the events being studied. The researcher is immersed in the setting so he/she can see, hear, feel, experience, subject's' daily life. There is concern about the potential bias of the researcher (observer bias) as an active participant. The researcher has to explain how bias is reduced or eliminated during the reporting of the data. Use of audiotapes and videotapes helps, in some respects, to guard against selective observations.

Unobtrusive or Non-participant Observation - researcher watches but does not participate in group activities.

Naturalistic Observation - observing individuals in their natural settings, making no effort to manipulate variables or control activities, but simply to observe and record.

Covert Observer - researcher disguises identity from other participants (ethical issues).

Differences in qualitative and quantitative observations

Quantitative observations use checklists with preliminary work done prior to the observation. Tally marks are generally used to identify behaviors. Qualitative observations use words to describe behaviors and attempt to describe what is happening in a context. [69]

- **Physical artifacts** refer to any physical evidence that might be gathered during fieldwork. That might include art work, notebooks, computer output, and other such physical evidence.
- **Interviews** are the most common method used by qualitative researchers. The method is used to gather information in the respondent or interviewee's own words from which insights on their interpretations can be obtained. The researcher encourages the interviewee to talk about their beliefs, experiences, feelings and perceptions concerning the phenomenon being studied. The type of interviews range from unstructured to totally structured interviews. Sørensen [69] outlines the different types as follows:

Unstructured – Appropriate for exploratory research. Questions are open-ended and impromptu questions are welcome. There is no structured format; hence it is flexible.

Partially Structured – Topic is chosen. Open-ended questions & responses are recorded nearly verbatim, possibly taped. Questions are formulated, but the order is up to the interviewer.

Semi-Structured – Questions and order of presentation are determined. Questions are open-ended, but the researcher records the essence of each response. Unstructured - exploratory, on a topic – open, flexible, no structured format, and impromptu questions

Structured – Questions and order are pre-determined; responses are coded by interviewer as they are given.

Totally structured – Questions, order, and coding are predetermined and the respondent is presented with alternatives for each question so that phrasing of responses is structured. Questions are self-coding in that each choice is pre-assigned a code.

Guidelines

- Listen more, talk less. Be Patient, Don't interrupt. Tolerate silence.
- Follow up on what participants say and ask questions when you don't understand.
- Don't be judgmental about participants' beliefs or views. You are there to learn about their perspectives whether you agree or not.
- Keep participants focused and ask for concrete details.
- Avoid leading questions, ask open ended questions.
- Don't debate with participants over their responses.
- You are a recorder, not a debater.

Differences in qualitative and quantitative interviews

Quantitative interviews are similar to "survey research" in that there are mainly fixed-choice questions and generally random samples. Interviews in qualitative studies are generally open-ended and generally use small, purposively selected samples.

Focus Group Discussion (FGD)

FGD is a carefully planned semi-structured discussion, moderated by a group leader and designed to obtain perceptions on a defined area of interest in a permissive non-threatening environment. FGD is relevant when insights are needed in exploratory studies and these insights can be used in preparation for a larger study. The method also enables the researcher to gain understanding of differences between groups. It is not useful when confidentiality cannot be assured; when the environment is emotionally charged; when other methodologies can produce better quality information; and when statistical projections are needed.

Guidelines

- Duration: 40 minutes-2 hours. General rule is to plan for less time than you tell participants.
- Number of Groups: 3-6 different groups should be used.
- Size: 4-12 with certain characteristics in common (Ideal size 6-8)
- Composition: Keep groups homogenous in terms of prestige or status.

Richard Boateng

Sampling in Qualitative Research

Sampling is a process of selecting samples from a group or population to become the foundation for studying a population in order to obtain data to address a research problem. A sample is a subset of a larger population. A population is a complete group of entities within which we want to explore, understand or predict a social phenomenon. Researchers make conclusions on a population by studying or investigating a sample. In QR, the objective of researchers is to study a phenomenon from the perspective of a sample that has experienced the phenomenon. QR is not about representativeness, it is more focused on samples which enhance understanding. Qualitative researchers use a non-probability sampling approach in which the probability of selecting any particular member is unknown. The sampling approach is non-random and sample size is generally small. This said, it is important for qualitative researchers to provide detailed information on how respondents or participants in a study where selected, including detailed descriptions of the participants, sample size and relevant characteristics (e.g. age, socioeconomic status, gender, etcetera) in respect of the study.

A primary challenge in qualitative research sampling is determining sample size: How many participants/cases are enough? The answer is 'It Depends'. First, the respondents should represent a range of potential respondents in order to ensure diversity in perspectives in data collected. Second, when the researcher reaches a point of data saturation, the same information is repeated from different participants. Hence, there is no need to engage any new participants/respondents in the study. Third, the research purpose and resource availability (For example, money and time) may influence access to participants and hence, constrain the sample size.

TYPES OF QUALITATIVE SAMPLING

The qualitative sampling techniques discussed by Zikmund [32], Neuman [2] and Sørensen [69] are outlined as follows:

- **Convenience Sample** - The sampling procedure of obtaining the people or units that are most conveniently available. Cases are obtained in any manner which is convenient. But there is a high possibility of the sample being ineffective and unrepresentative; hence this sampling method is not always advisable [32] [2].
- **Purposive Sample** - An experienced individual selects the sample based on the researcher's judgment about some appropriate characteristics required of the sample. It is often used in exploratory research, for selecting particular cases for in-depth investigation, or for selecting members which are often difficult to reach [32] [2].
- **Purposeful Random Sample** – Sample is first selected purposively and second, randomly selected within the purposive sample. This happens when the purposive sample is too numerous to include all in the study [69].
- **Stratified Purposeful Sample** - Selection based on subgroups; several cases at each of the several levels of variation of the phenomenon [69].
- **Theory-based or Operational Construct Sample** - Sampling by choosing units to fit the theoretical constructs [69].
- **Snowball or Chain Sample** - It is a multistage sampling technique – beginning with a few people and growing through referral. Initial respondents are selected by other methods like purposive sampling or random sampling. Additional respondents are obtained from information provided by the initial respondents [32] [2].
- **Extreme or Deviant Case** - Searching cases that differ from the dominant pattern. Researchers use various techniques to identify cases with specific characteristics that differ from the dominant [32] [2]. For example, school dropouts who seem not to have a record of illegal activities and who are stable from two-parent, upper-middle income families.

Other qualitative sampling techniques discussed by Sørensen [69]:

- **Opportunistic Sample** - Selecting participants based on taking advantage of unexpected situations.
- **Politically Important Sample** - Selection of participants who are well known and would create wide interest in the study.
- **Confirming and Disconfirming Case Sample** - Selection of participants to look for variation or exceptions; confirming cases are selected to confirm patterns, themes or meanings found in previous cases; disconfirming cases are selected because they are believed to be likely to disconfirm previous findings.
- **Criterion Sample** - Selecting all cases that meet some criteria or have particular characteristics (e.g. students who have been retained for two consecutive years, female administrators with more than 20 years of experience).
- **Homogeneous Sample** - Selecting participants who are very similar in experiences, perspectives, or outlook to produce a narrow sample and make collection and analysis simpler.

Structuring the Methodology Section of a Research Paper and Dissertation

In this section, I present exhibits of methodology sections from qualitative research papers and dissertations. The objective is to provide researchers and students with some direction in structuring the methodology section of their write-ups. However, before I present the exhibits, I want to briefly explain some usually confusing terminologies associated with research methodology.

RESEARCH METHODOLOGY VS RESEARCH METHODS AND RESEARCH STRATEGY VS RESEARCH DESIGN

Research methodology refers to the framework used to conduct a research, within the context of a particular research paradigm (set of philosophical assumptions) [70]. This can be contrasted from a **research method** which characterizes the set of specific tools and techniques used to gather and analyze the data as specified by the research methodology. Hence, a research method, for instance an interview, can be used in different research methodologies (quantitative, qualitative and mixed-methods). Each research methodology has a number of strategies, as ways of carrying out research within that methodology. Qualitative research has a number of **research strategies** including case study, phenomenology, and grounded theory. For each of these strategies, the researcher is required to develop a **research design** which describes how, when and where data is to be collected and how the data will be analyzed.

TYPES OF MIXED-METHODS RESEARCH

Mixed-methods approach tends to combine the strengths of both qualitative and quantitative approaches to conduct a research. However, there is sometimes confusion about how mixed methods research is carried out. Creswell explains three types of mixed-methods research approaches (extract below) [71]:

Sequential mixed methods procedures are those in which the researcher seeks to elaborate on or expand on the findings of one method with another method. This may involve beginning with a qualitative interview for exploratory purposes and following up with a quantitative, survey method with a large sample so that the researcher can generalize results to a population. Alternatively, the study may begin with a quantitative method in which a theory or concept is tested, followed by a qualitative method involving detailed exploration with a few cases or individuals.

Concurrent mixed methods procedures are those in which the researcher converges or merges quantitative and qualitative data in order to provide a comprehensive analysis of the research problem. In this design, the investigator collects both forms of data at the same time and then integrates the information in the interpretation of the overall results. Also, in this design, the researcher may embed one smaller form of data within another larger data collection in order to analyze different types of questions (the qualitative addresses the process while the quantitative, the outcomes).

Transformative mixed methods procedures are those in which the researcher uses a theoretical lens as an overarching perspective within a design that contains both quantitative and qualitative data. This lens provides a framework for topics of interest, methods for collecting data, and outcomes or changes anticipated by the study. Within this lens could be a data collection method that involves a sequential or a concurrent approach.

EXHIBITS OF RESEARCH METHODOLOGY

As a fairly structured guideline for research methodology, a researcher is required to:

(1) Identify and state a research paradigm for the research (optional, rarely stated but may be deduced from the data collection process. It is necessary for PhD research and some MPhil research).

(2) Identify and explain the choice of a particular methodological approach (qualitative, quantitative and mixed-methods).

(3) Identify and explain the choice of a particular research strategy in respect of the choice of methodology.

(4) Identify the population, sampling method and sample size.

(5) What methods were used to conduct the study and why were those methods selected? In systematic fashion you need to explain how data was collected.

- Context – where are study subjects located?
- Unit of Analysis – What level of Analysis: Meta, Macro, Meso, or Micro (individual)
- Data Collection Methods – primary data (observed and collected in person) and secondary (recorded, documented evidence)

(6) You need to explain in brief how you analyzed the data and dug out themes or answers or key lessons from your findings.

Examples of research methodology sections are showcased in Exhibits 40 - 42.

Richard Boateng

Exhibit 35 Research Methodology - Example 1

Advancing E-commerce Beyond Readiness in a Developing Country:
This study intends to understand the dynamics of the readiness factors in Ghanaian firms' adoption and conduct of e-commerce. There was therefore a strong case for using an exploratory case study method since this supports the research objective set out at the beginning (Yin 2003). In order to get the richness of experiences and undertake an in-depth investigation, the multiple-case study method was followed (Yin, 2003). In a case study research, there is no universally acceptable number of cases and a case study research could be based on a single case or many cases (Walsham, 1993; Yin, 2003). This is because the validity of the case study has more to do with the "plausibility and cogency of the logical reasoning" (Walsham, 1993:15) and less with the number of cases. In addition, the validity of case studies can be enhanced by the strategic selection of cases rather than their number (De Vaus, 2001). Therefore, this study is based on evidence collected from 10 major cases and 15 other organizations. .

The data collected consisted of personal interviews with 28 individuals, across 25 different Ghanaian companies, educational institutions and industrial associations involved in e-commerce development in Ghana. This was done in the interest of triangulating data sources. Triangulation provides a unique opportunity to identify inconsistent and contradictory evidence which researchers should analyze and interpret carefully (Mathison, 1988). Concerning the interviews, organizations selected were obtained from The Ghana Club 100 and referrals from Internet Service Providers (ISPs), academics and ICT graduates from the Ghana-India Kofi Annan Centre of Excellence in ICT. The Ghana Club 100 is an annual compilation of the top 100 companies in Ghana to give recognition to successful enterprise building (GC100, 2004). 35 Ghana Club 100 organizations, covering manufacturing, trading services, and financial sectors, were selected. Only 10 of the 35 organizations responded when contacted. A total of 13 interviews were done across the 10 firms.

15 other organizations, who were not listed in the Ghana Club 100, contributed our remaining 15 interviews. They include 4 Internet Service Providers (ISPs); 4 ICT consultancies; the Ghana Export Promotion Council; 3 non-traditional export firms; the National Communication Authority (NCA) (the regulator of the telecommunication sector); and two academics from two Ghanaian tertiary institutions with expert knowledge on the Ghanaian ICT sector. The representative from NCA and the two academics were interviewed to verify and obtain other perspectives on data obtained from selected firms and ISPs.

The interviews were recorded and transcribed, with copies of transcribed interviews returned to interviewees to check and resolve discrepancies. The interviews were also collaborated with data from documentary materials including past e-commerce project documentation in the selected firms' industry reports, verified media accounts and statistical databases. The interview transcription and analysis was done with the aid of ATLAS.ti®software, a qualitative analysis software. The software was used as a data administration and archiving tool for the thematic analysis of the transcribed interviews. Themes from our research framework guided the codification of the text in the transcribed interviews. The interviews consisted of open-ended questions about the government, technology, market and cultural readiness factors which affect the implementation of electronic commerce in Ghana. Interviews were modified to be relevant to the industry in which the interviewee worked in. Interviewees identified the challenges relevant to their firms and experiences in e-commerce adoption and the ICT sector. Other questions inquired about how they addressed the challenges and suggestions on how to sustain e-commerce benefits. Source: [72]

EXHIBIT 36 RESEARCH METHODOLOGY - EXAMPLE 2

Mobiles and Micro-trading – Conceptualizing the Link

The study seeks to investigate the impact of mobile phones on micro-trading activities of women traders in Ghana. A mixed methods approach consisting of a survey and case study was adopted in order to explore the consistency of findings and obtain richness and detail to understand how mobiles phones impact micro-trading activities (Creswell, 2003). A survey was conducted to explore the mobile phone usage behavior of 136 traders. A follow-up case study was conducted with 4 traders to develop an in-depth understanding of mobile usage behavior and gain insight into observations from the survey. An exploratory case study approach was adopted since it strongly supports the research objective set at the beginning (Yin, 1994). This research also sought to benefit from the rigors of designing, collecting and analyzing data as discussed by De Vaus (2001). The mixed methods approach enabled us to develop propositions on the mobile phone usage behavior of the traders.

The data was collected over a four-month period. Three sets of interviews were conducted. The first set of interviews was conducted with women traders. A questionnaire was structured to reflect the framework presented in Figure 1. A sample size of 150 was chosen from two markets – Kaneshie and Abogbloshie – in Accra, capital city of Ghana. Out of the 150, 136 were successfully administered, representing a 91% response rate. 77 (56%) respondents were from Kaneshie market and 59 (44%) from Abogbloshie market. Data from the survey was analyzed through descriptive statistics using SPSS. The second set of interviews was conducted with four traders randomly selected from the Madina and Makola markets for an in-depth study of their micro-trading activities. The objective was to get a representation of traders across the four major markets in Accra and also capture rich mobile and trading experiences from different markets. Two case studies from the four interviews are presented in this paper. The third set of interviews was conducted with four of the marketing personnel of two mobile network operators in Ghana, and two resellers of mobile pre-paid cards and mobile accessories. There are currently 5 major network operators in Ghana, namely: MTN, TiGO, Zain, Kasapa, and Vodafone. The interviews were conducted with marketing personnel from TiGO, Zain and resellers of prepaid cards and mobile accessories with respect to the services that have become beneficial to traders. The interviews in both sets of interviews were recorded and transcribed, with copies of transcribed interviews sent to the interviewees to check and resolve discrepancies.

The approach to analyzing the case study was primarily by use of pattern-matching logic as explained by Yin (1994). We sought for results that can strengthen the validity of our theoretical framework, further by scrutinizing the context of the case and detailing findings to provide answers to the research question. Source: [19]

EXHIBIT 37 RESEARCH METHODOLOGY - EXAMPLE 3

Perceived Knowledge, Skills and Attitude (KSA) of Health Care Professionals towards Health Information Systems in Ghana: The Case of University of Cape Coast Hospital

4.1 Introduction

The research methodology included; research design, case setting, research population, sampling techniques and sample size, data collection instrument and method, data processing and mode of analysis, variables, and ethical considerations.

4.2 Research Design

The purpose of the research is to investigate health care professionals' perceived KSA towards the usage of the HIS in provision of information for the planning and management of health services in a University health care institution. To achieve this research purpose, hypotheses based upon the Technology Acceptance Model (TAM) (Davis, 1989) were developed. A combination of quantitative and qualitative approaches - case study and survey - was employed for this study. A case study was conducted to document the context of the health sector in Ghana and the profile of the University of Cape Coast Hospital. A cross-sectional, descriptive survey design was used to collect data needed to answer research questions according to the guidelines provided by Yin (2003). The study collected in-depth description of the knowledge, skills and attitude of university health care professionals towards HIS by employing some descriptive statistics. Besides using mainly questionnaires, interviewing, and observations the study also relied on secondary documentation such as facility action plan, and reports for case findings and other details of the hospital.

4.3 Study and Target Population

The study population included all health professionals employed by the University of Cape Coast hospital; before and during the time data was collected. The target population was management members, as well as technical staff from the Records and Pharmacy units of the hospital, who were extensive users of the HIS in the facility. They included Biostatisticians, Records clerks, Pharmacy Technicians, and some administrative staff. This was due to the assumption that they were free from bias in telling about the HIS system used in the facility. The exclusion criteria related to health professionals whose work procedures had no link at all to the usage or management of the HIS in the facility, during the study, period were excluded from the study.

4.4 Sampling Techniques and Sample Size

At the time of the study, there were four (4) existing functional University Hospitals in Ghana including; University of Cape Coast (UCC) Hospital, University of Ghana-Legon (UG) Hospital, Kwame Nkrumah University of Science and Technology (KNUST) Hospital (Kumasi), and the University of Education Winneba (UEW) Hospital. These academic health facilities not only serve students, staff and their dependents, but also the university communities and their general environs as well as the public. For this study, a convenient sampling procedure; which is a non-probability sampling technique, was used to select UCC Hospital as the study case setting. The academic health facility is in the context of the study as background information indicates that it recently shifted from using manual systems to using HISs to support the delivery of health care. Moreover, the facility which is located in the central regional capital of Ghana is where the researcher resides, favoring proximity and ability to gain access to the facility and study subjects.

Purposive sampling technique; which is also a non-probability sampling technique, was employed in selecting thirty (30) health care professionals from the Records and Pharmacy units who were technical staff and directly associated with the usage of the HIS in the hospital. Sample size in this study depended mainly on what could be done with available time and resources, and the exclusion criteria as far as the usage of the HIS was concerned. The subdivision of the technical respondents included seventeen (17) and thirteen (13) Records and Pharmacy staff respectively. In addition, five (5) questionnaires were administered on management members of the hospital, including the Director, Administrator, Accountant, Nurse Manager and Pharmacist. In total, thirty-five (35) questionnaires were administered on the University of Cape Coast Hospital staff for the purposes of the study.

4.5 Variables

The variables to be studied included socio-demographic and professional characteristics, computer literacy, perceived knowledge, skills on HIS usage, and attitude towards HIS usage. Other variables included Perceived Ease of Use (PEOU) and Perceived Usefulness (PU) of the system, which are referred to as determinants of the TAM model.

4.6 Data Collection Instrument and Method

In an attempt to address research questions and to find out facts or opinions or both for that matter, the data collection instrument employed for this study was a questionnaire. An initial draft of the questionnaire was developed based on research objectives and literature review, as well as expert opinion. It consisted of questions to identify and measure university healthcare professionals' perceived knowledge, skills and attitude, towards the use of HIS in health care delivery and services. The questionnaire instrument contained eight (8) parts; which included socio-demographic characteristics and professional background (Part I), perceived knowledge on HIS usage (Part II), skills and HIS usage (Part III), perceived ease of use (Part IV), perceived usefulness (Part V), attitude towards HIS usage (Part VI), management support (Part VII), and general comments (Part VIII). All questions; except those in the socio-demographic characteristics and professional background and general comments sections, captured responses via a five point Likert scale with responses ranging from "Strongly Disagree (SD)" to "Strongly Agree (SA)". Questions in the perceived ease of use, perceived usefulness, and attitude about HIS usage sections assessed variables endogenous to the technology acceptance model (TAM).

A pilot test was conducted on health professionals at the University of Ghana Hospital to ensure clarity of the questionnaire, to check face validity, reliability and test-retest reliability. Pilot testing was necessary to determine the average length of time needed to complete the survey, as well as how to manage and analyze the data collected. University of Ghana (UG) Hospital is based in Accra, and is one of the largest healthcare providers in the Ghanaian capital. It is similar to the study population in several ways. Its urban location, types of services provided and academic affiliation make it relatively comparable to the University of Cape Coast Hospital. The pilot site is, however, dissimilar to the study population in some ways. Health professionals practicing in the UG health facility have not been using HIS as part of their everyday practice for many years. Their responses are likely to be different than those received from the study population, as HIS has been implemented within the UCC health facility for a number of years. It was not anticipated that these dissimilarities would impact the outcomes of the final study, as the pilot health professionals were able to accurately evaluate the instrument and provide valuable feedback regarding the survey items. A revised version of the questionnaire was then structured and prepared for self-administering. A letter was sent to management of UCC Hospital informing them of the research and seeking their support to ensure that all staff members concerned received a communication about the potential to be selected to participate in the exercise. Subsequently, health care professionals at UCC Hospital were purposively selected, and given a self-completion questionnaire for the study. The questionnaire included a covering brief introduction, explaining the nature of the study and confirmation that recipients retained full control over the decision to complete the questionnaire or not.

Ethical issues were addressed considering various precautionary approaches. An introductory letter of permission to obtain data/information was obtained from the Department of Operations and Management

Information Systems (OMIS) University of Ghana Business School (UGBS). The purpose and objectives of the study were concisely explained to the target respondents. The confidentiality of their responses was clearly explained for the appreciation of the respondents. Finally, health care professionals were involved only after informed consent was obtained, and were alerted that it was their right to participate or not (entirely voluntary), and moreover their involvement did not have anything to do with their job evaluation. It was emphasized that their response was entirely voluntary.

4.7 Data Processing and Mode of Analysis

Data was organized and processed using Statistical Package for Social Scientists (SPSS) version 16.0 and Microsoft Office Excel 2007. Descriptive statistics including frequency tables, simple percentages, measures of central tendency and dispersions were compiled. The test statistic for the hypothesis testing was Correlation analysis, which is the process of measuring the nature and strength of relationship between variables. There are several correlation coefficients for measuring various types of relationships between different kinds of measurements, but this study used the Pearson correlation coefficient (r), which is one of the more widely used correlation coefficients according to experts.

4.8 Chapter Summary

The chapter discussed the research design, the study and target population, sampling techniques and sample size, the variables under study, the data collection instrument and methodology, and then data processing and mode of analysis. Source: [73]

Summary

In designing a research study, researchers need to identify whether they will employ a qualitative, quantitative, or mixed methods design. In this chapter we explained one of the approaches, qualitative research. After deciding the research methodology researchers have to decide on the research strategy, thus making a choice among the methods discussed in the chapter. Case study seems to be most common method. Beyond the research strategy the researcher has to select an appropriate sampling technique and relevant data collection methods to obtain the data required to understand the phenomenon under study. The methods and techniques used should be well-documented and logically presented in the methodology section of the researcher's write-up.

In the next chapter we will discuss qualitative data analysis.

Chapter Discussion

QUESTION 1

Discuss five of the twelve principles of qualitative research espoused by Patton [51].

QUESTION 2

Discuss two qualitative research strategies and describe how they have been used in your discipline of study.

CHAPTER 7

Qualitative
Data analysis

Objectives

This chapter seeks to discuss qualitative data analysis methods for qualitative research. These methods include Miles and Huberman's Data Analysis Approach and Yin's Data Analysis Approach. It will also explain within case analysis and cross-case analysis, and how to present arguments in qualitative writing[7].

---

7 Picture source: http://infolytics.wordpress.com/category/data-analysis/

Qualitative Data Analysis

A NUMBER OF qualitative data analysis techniques have been discussed in literature. In this chapter we will discuss the techniques posited by Miles and Huberman [48] [74] and Yin [75] [60]. Quite a number of other researchers tend to propose other techniques, using the works of these authors as a basis. Schutt [76] presents a summary of the different techniques that are shared by most approaches to qualitative data analysis (Exhibit 38):

- Documentation of the data and the process of data collection;
- Organization/categorization of the data into concepts;
- Connection of the data to show how one concept may influence another;
- Corroboration/legitimization, by evaluating alternative explanations, disconfirming evidence, and searching for negative cases; and
- Representing the account (reporting the findings).

EXHIBIT 38 FLOW MODEL OF QUALITATIVE DATA ANALYSIS COMPONENTS

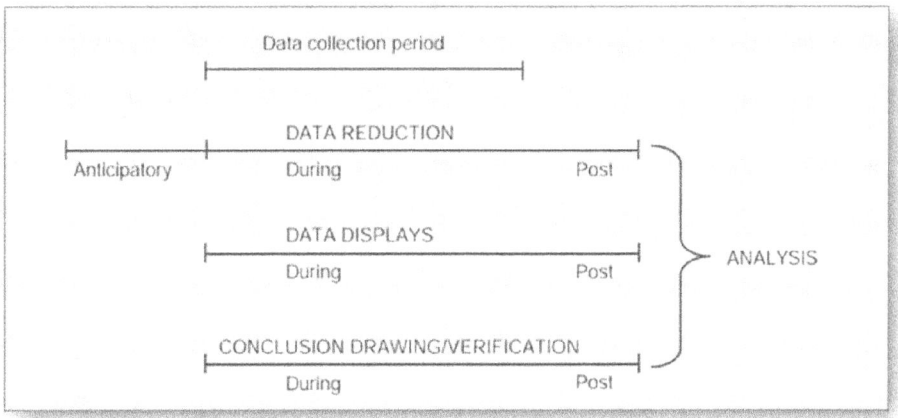

Source: [76]

In this chapter, I will discuss the components of data analysis in qualitative research with a primary focus on Miles and Huberman's Data Analysis Approach supported by the arguments and explanations summarized by Schutt [76].

Miles and Huberman Data Analysis Approach

EXHIBIT 39 MILES AND HUBERMAN'S DATA ANALYSIS APPROACH

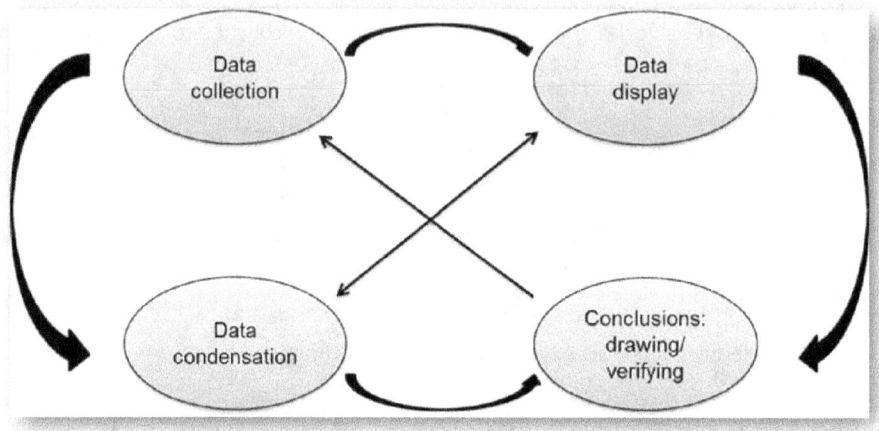

Source: [74]

As illustrated in the above exhibit, Miles and Huberman propose an iterative data analysis approach starting from data reduction [48]. However, it was changed because data reduction implies "weakening or losing something in the process. The process continues to Data Display and Conclusions: drawing and verifying. I will briefly explain each of the three main steps but beginning with Data Collection.

DATA COLLECTION

Prior to data reduction, the researcher is required to collect data. Whiles collecting data, the analysis begins. The researcher is encouraged to take notes and read through them to sort out and categorize the data in respect of its relevance to the different respondents/contacts and to the research questions to be addressed. Notes can be done on the margins of questionnaires and research notebook or diary; especially key concepts – new or confirming – are identified in the data collection process. Thus, identification and summarization should begin during the time of observation and interviewing [76]. During my PhD, my supervisor sent an email reminding me of this important step, as I was totally immersed in my data collection and barely concerned about doing a concurrent analysis of the data I was collecting. Effective and consistent note taking during the data collection helps to make the analysis less daunting, especially since the researcher is less likely to have a perfect recollection of events after the data collection has been completed. Anderson shares from personal experience that

> Usually, I wrote these notes immediately after spending time in the setting or the next day. Through the exercise of writing up my field notes, with attention to "who" the speakers and actors were, I became aware of the nature of certain social relationships and their positional arrangements within the peer group. (Anderson 2003:235)

Anderson's personal experiences reiterate the fact that analysis begins when note taking and daily reflections on data collection activities begin. To keep track of observations and interviews, who and what occurred during data collection, Miles and Huberman [48] suggest the use of a contact summary form (Exhibit 40).

EXHIBIT 40 CONTACT SUMMARY TEMPLATE

Contact type: _____ Visit: _____ Phone: _____ (with whom)	Site: Contact date: Today's date: Written by:	
1. What were the main issues or themes that struck you in this contact?		
2. Summarize the information you got (or failed to get) on each of the target questions you had for this contact.		
Question	**Information**	
Question 1		
Question 2		
Question 3		
3. Anything else that struck you as salient, interesting, illuminating or important in this contact?		
4. What new (or remaining) target questions do you have in considering the next contact with this site?		

Source: [48]

DATA CONDENSATION

Data condensation refers to the "process of selecting, focusing, simplifying, abstracting, and/or transforming the data that appear in the full corpus (body) of written-up field notes, interview transcripts, documents, and other empirical materials" [74]. Data condensation starts at the very initial research phase and continues throughout the analysis. The early stages begin with editing, segmenting and summarizing data. In the middle stages, the researcher progresses to coding and memoing to find themes, clusters and patterns. In the latter stages, the researcher begins to conceptualize and explain to draw out abstract concepts. Within these activities, the researcher should not strip data from its context – thus data should be condensed without losing key information which support explanations and give evidence.

Early Stages

It is important to understand that data condensation activities are iterative – it may begin with a "simple observation that is interpreted directly, 'pulled apart', and then put back together more meaningfully" [76]. Condensation makes data stronger [74]. Condensation does not necessarily require or mean quantification – the condensation can be done in many ways including:

- Through summary or paraphrase: when the essence of a conservation or an interview is presented rather than the actual words used in the conservation or an interview. Summary can also be used when a series of statements tend to emphasize the same point.
- Through being subsumed in a larger pattern: when a series of actions tend to depict a behavior. For example, absenteeism from class may be viewed as the behavior of a student who has failed to show up in class three times consecutively.
- Examining the magnitude: when the researcher examines an occurrence in a scale – high or low degree of effectiveness / or high or low rate of absenteeism.

Coding

Coding refers to the condensation of data into meaningful segments and assigning names (labels) to the segments [48]. In essence, it is the process of putting tags, names or labels against pieces of data and thereafter, combining the codes into broader categories or themes. However, what are codes? Codes are tags, names or labels. The purpose of data is to index data to become the foundation for new data in future analysis and also to develop/identify patterns that explain social phenomena.

Miles and Huberman [48] identified two types of codes: descriptive and pattern codes. In relation, Richards [77] also proposes two types: topic and analytic codes. Descriptive codes store information describing an event, activity, behavior or phenomenon being studied. Topic codes are labels assigned according to a subject; hence they tend to be descriptive in nature. Inferential or pattern codes pull together information including descriptive/topic codes into more meaningful units. Pattern codes focus on interpreting, interconnecting and conceptualizing data. Other forms of coding often used in grounded theory are classified as [78]:

In vivo codes – focus on what is in the data
Open Codes – raises the conceptual level of data
Axial Codes – focus on Interconnections between open codes
Selective Codes – raises the conceptual level of data again

In closer examination, the first level of coding irrespective of the classification is descriptive and the second and higher levels are analytic.

STAGE ONE – OPEN CODING

The data is carefully read, all statements relating to the research question are identified, and each is assigned a code, or category. These codes are then noted, and each relevant statement is organized under its appropriate code. Data can be coded either through a theory-driven approach (deductive) – where prespecified codes from literature or theory guide the coding process; or a data-driven approach (inductive) – where the first set of codes is derived from the data. The latter approach relies on a coding scheme after initial analysis. However, the two approaches are not an either-or decision; they are both relevant in any coding process. An example of coding is illustrated in Exhibit 41.

Exhibit 41 An Example of Coding Reponses

PhD Supervision Experiences in University of Lakien
Student 1: 'Supervisors are usually World Bank experts and very knowledgeable but often away for global assignments'

Code: Knowledgeable supervisors

Student 2: 'I spent more time on Skype for discussions with my supervisor'

Code: Limited Face-to-face interaction

The codes developed from data have to have three characteristics:

- **Valid**: codes should accurately reflect what is being researched.
- **Mutually exclusive**: codes should be distinct, with no overlap.
- **Exhaustive**: all relevant data should fit into a code.

Researchers may begin with an initial deductive approach – starting with their theoretical framework and wider literature. Afterwards, a coding framework may be developed with clear operational definitions so that subsequent coding is much easier. The codes developed at this stage are primarily descriptive.

Stage Two – Axial and Pattern Coding

Using the codes developed in stage 1, the researcher rereads the qualitative data, and searches for statements that may fit into any of the categories and be grouped into more meaningful and general patterns. Throughout this stage, codes can be removed, revised and re-categorized into sub-codes as more data is being examined (inductive approach).

A number of key questions may be asked, such as: What is happening here? Is there anything here which is not directly observable? What are the similarities? What are the differences? The researcher is not only examining the similarities but also the idiosyncrasies and differences. Further, the researcher should become more analytical, and look for patterns and explanation in the codes. Questions should be asked such as [79]:

- Can I relate certain codes together under a more general code?
- Can I organize codes sequentially (For example, does code A happen before code B)?
- Can I identify any causal relationships (does code A cause code B)?

This process may take quite a number of iterations before the researcher can progress to the next stage.

Stage Three – Selective Coding
This stage involves reading through the raw data for cases that illustrate the analysis, or explain the concepts. The researcher has to look for contradictory and confirmatory data. The researcher should avoid looking for data that only confirms the ideas of the researcher.

Parallel Stage: Memoing
Alongside coding the researcher is required to create memos. Memoing is the process of theorizing the "write-up of ideas about codes and their relationships as they strike the analyst while coding..." [78]. A memo is created when data (as sentence, paragraph or few pages) finds links with theory and previous literature discussion. There is a need to record all ideation (link with literature or theory) when they happen and as they happen, as memos. The link can either be confirmatory or contradictory [78] (see Exhibit 42). The researcher moves from the descriptive and empirical level to the conceptual level. As such, memoing characterizes the initial steps towards the development of propositions.

Exhibit 42 An Example of Memoing

Example of Confirmatory Memoing
Title: Mobiles and Micro-trading Activities – Conceptualizing the Link
In Case A, AA uses her phone's calendar functionality to schedule the times to supply her customers who need tomatoes. In Case B, customers are able to monitor delivery times of goods and plan for contingencies through text messages.

This communication medium creates a borderless environment or redefines the "place" factor in transacting business with customers and creating more personalized services for them. Personalized services lead to deepened relationships which can contribute to customer loyalty and retention. **Williamson (1981) refers to this phenomenon of 'deepened relationships' as asset specificity**, a transaction characteristic which depicts customers 'locked into' a transaction for a considerable time.

Example of Contradictory Memoing
Title: Mobiles and Micro-trading Activities – Conceptualizing the Link
The traders predominantly used mobile phones to improve existing trading activities. These include the communication and information exchange with customers and trading partners through the use of voice calls and text messages. Little can be said about the transformational impact of mobile phones. **Contrary to previous research** on mobile phones usage by fishermen and farmers in Ghana (Boadi *et al.*, 2007), there is no evidence of the use of mobile banking services in these micro-trading activities. This finding, perhaps, stems from the differences in the economic volume and type of transactions involved in fishing and farming as compared to micro-trading activities of the traders interviewed in this research.

Source: [19]

DATA DISPLAY

A "display is an organized, compressed assembly of information that allows conclusion drawing" [74]. Displays may be in the form of graphs, charts, tables, networks, tabulating the frequency of events, ordering the information, and diagrams of different types (venn diagrams and causal models) (see Exhibits 43 and 44). They may also include extracts from online applications like Facebook Status, software interfaces and any other photo exhibits which are relevant to explaining the codes or patterns found in data. Display organizes and summarizes the data to help establish/explain themes, and also becomes the basis for future analysis. During my PhD, I used data display to explain the business processes in the case study of a Ghanaian used-car retailer.

EXHIBIT 43 AN EXAMPLE OF DATA DISPLAY USING PROCESS DIAGRAM

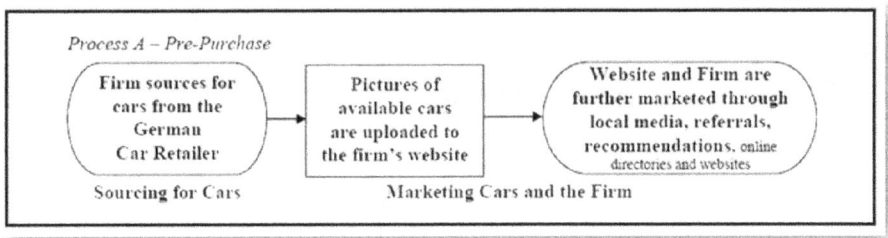

Exhibit 44 An Example of Data Display Using a Table for Comparison

	Internal Resources	External Resources	Concurring Previous IS and E-commerce Research
Assets	Financial readiness		Grandon and Pearson (2004); Kuan and Chau (2001)
	IS infrastructure – Pentium I and II computers		Feeny and Willocks (1998) Wade and Hulland (2004)
Ordinary Capabilities		Changing national ICT context (dial-up Internet services and cybercafés)	Montealegre (2002) Okoli and Mbarika (2003)
		Use of resources abroad	Montealegre (2002) Wresch (2003)
	IS project management		Boateng and Molla (2006) Jarvenpaa and Leidner (2003)

Conclusion Drawing/Verification

During data condensation and display some tentative or first-level/early conclusions may be identified. However, these conclusions have to be verified once they have been formed. Miles and Huberman outlined 13 tactics for drawing meaning and conclusions and another 13 tactics for testing and confirming findings. These tactics are guidelines to help researchers. Verified conclusions become the propositions which stem from the research study. Researchers are advised to hold all early conclusions lightly, maintaining openness and skepticism, but with potential to become more established or finalized, as these meanings are tested for the plausibility, representativeness, triangulation and other criteria outlined in Exhibit 45.

Exhibit 45 Tactics for Conclusion Drawing and Verification

Tactics for Generating Meaning

i.   Noting Patterns and themes

ii.   Seeing Plausibility

iii.   Seeing Clustering - what goes with what

iv.   Making Metaphors - integration in diverse pieces of data

v.   Counting - to see what is there

vi.   Making Contrasts/comparisons

vii.   Partitioning Variables

viii.   Subsuming Particulars into the General

ix.   Factoring

x.   Noting Relationships between Variables

xi.   Finding Intervening Variables

xii.   Building a Logical Chain of Evidence

xiii.   Making Conceptual/theoretical coherence

Testing and Confirming Meanings

i.   Checking for Representativeness

ii.   Checking for Researcher Effects

iii.   Triangulating Data Sources

iv.   Weighting the Evidence

v.   Checking the Meaning of outliers

vi.   Using Extreme Cases

vii.   Following up Surprises

viii.   Looking for Negative Evidence

ix.   Making If-Then Tests

x.   Ruling out Spurious Relations

xi.   Replicating a Finding

xii.   Checking out Rival Explanations

xiii.   Getting Feedback from Informants

Qualitative data analysis is not a linear process and requires many, many iterations. The propositions may be stated as lessons and used to explain or develop models concerning the phenomenon under study (see Exhibit 46).

Exhibit 46 Example of Conclusion Drawing and Verifying

Title: Mobiles and Micro-trading Activities – Conceptualizing the Link

....the innovative use of calculators in trading was observed. 12 out of the 18 traders with no formal education claimed to use calculators in trading activities, primarily in post and during-trade activities. 8 out of the 18 traders with no formal education also claimed to use text messaging in contacting trading partners and customers. This ability to identify basic functions in mobile phones and integrate them in trading activities is arguably a function of some level of education and the perceived ease of using the mobile phones they owned. On further enquiry, these traders intimated that they often received help from their children, friends, relatives and sometimes customers in learning some of the functions of mobile phones, especially with 'simple' text messages, calculators, and the use of calendars as reminders. The perceived ease-of-use was influenced by the mobile literacy of these traders which stemmed from informal education or knowledge dispersion through social networks. The knowledge dispersion through social networks, however, iterates the blurred distinctions between the social and productive (business) spheres in the adoption and usage of mobile phones (Rangaswamy and Nair, 2010). These findings are suggestive of the first lesson:

Lesson One: *The innovative use of mobile phones in micro-trading is influenced by the pre-knowledge of the trader which may have been developed through formal education and/or social networks.*

Source: [19]

Yin's Data Analysis Approach

Yin [80] presented five analytic techniques applicable to case study research: pattern-matching, explanation-building, cross-case synthesis, logic, and time-series analysis. Only the first three techniques are discussed in this book. To begin, the analysis of a case study relies on an analytical framework. The analytical framework can exist in two forms. First, the researcher can use the theoretical propositions that led to the case study (see [81]). If theoretical propositions are not present, then second, the researcher could consider developing a descriptive framework around which the case study is organized. The researcher would therefore develop a case description, which would become the framework for organizing the case study.

PATTERN-MATCHING

This analytical technique aims to link data to propositions. It uses comparison to explore or determine the relationships between empirically-based patterns and predicted patterns (propositions) [82]. If the patterns match, the internal reliability of the study is enhanced. Researchers conducting descriptive case studies are required to propose the predicted patterns before the case study is developed. However, in explanatory case studies the patterns may be related to the dependent or the independent variables of the study (or both) [80]. For further reference, Yin [60] provides an exhaustive discussion on how to identify and develop patterns in different scenarios including single and multiple case studies.

EXPLANATION-BUILDING

This analytical technique is arguably a form of pattern-matching. Explanation requires the stipulation of a set of causal links about a phenomenon, or "how" or "why" something happened [80]. It is "an iterative process that begins with a theoretical statement refines it, revises the proposition, and repeats this process from the beginning" [68]. The iteration may entail [80]:

- Making an initial theoretical statement or an initial proposition about policy or social behavior;
- Comparing the findings of an initial case against such a statement or proposition;
- Revising the statement or proposition;

- Comparing other details of the case against the revision;
- Comparing the revision to the facts of a second, third, or more cases; and
- Repeating this process as many times as is needed.

The process may continue until the researcher builds an explanation of the case. It is arguably most useful in explanatory case studies, though it is possible to be used for exploratory cases to develop hypotheses. It is argued that some researchers lose focus or drift away from the research purpose in the iterative quest for explanation. Hence, Yin [80] advises that the researcher should have a consistent focus on the original purpose of the inquiry and the possible alternative explanations that may help to reduce this potential problem. .

CROSS-CASE SYNTHESIS

A cross-case synthesis is an analytical technique for multiple case studies. The previous techniques discussed can be used with either single- or multiple-case studies. Multiple case studies tend to strengthen explanations or conclusions made by case study research [80]. The multiple case studies can be compared through the creation of word tables to display the data from the individual cases according to some uniform framework (see Exhibit 47). Cross-case patterns will rely strongly on argumentative interpretation, not numeric tallies. The researcher can probe the similarities and differences between the cases to develop naturalistic generalizations[8] from analyzing the data; generalizations that can be drawn from the case for application by the subjects under study or to apply to a population of cases.

For large numbers of individual case studies, Yin advises the incorporation of quantitative techniques in the syntheses. Quantitative techniques can be used to summarize and compare the variation of constructs in relation to the explanation from the qualitative analysis.

---

8 Stake (1995) "naturalistic generalizations are conclusions arrived at through personal engagement in life's affairs or by vicarious experience so well constructed that the person feels as if it happened to themselves (p. 85)."

Exhibit 47 Example of Cross-Case Syntheses

	Case A	Case B
Time Period	Jan 2005 – Jul 2007	Jan 2002 – Jul 2007
Assets	Financial readiness Use of resources abroad *New key staff – Internet strategist* *IS infrastructure* *Broadband Internet*	Production infrastructure Financial readiness Use of resources abroad *New key staff – executives and IT personnel* *IS infrastructure* *Broadband Internet*
Ordinary Capabilities	Changing national ICT context IS project management *IT-vendor relationship*	Changing national ICT context IS project management *IT-vendor relationship*
Core Capabilities	Social capital for offline marketing Partnership with German car retailer *Partnership with financial institutions*	Social capital for offline marketing *Strategic focus on core objective – production, marketing and promotion of products.*

Stake's Within Case Analysis

Beyond cross-case syntheses, there is also within-case analysis for single case studies. This analysis consists of making a detailed description of the case and its setting. According to Stake [65], the analysis can be done in two steps - categorical aggregation and direct interpretation. In categorical aggregation, the researcher explores data to identify a collection of instances from which issues relevant to the study will emerge. The issues may be categorized for further analysis of establishing patterns and interconnections between two or more categories. In direct interpretation, on the other hand, the researcher identifies a single instance and draws meaning from it without looking for multiple stances.

ENHANCING QUALITY OF ANALYSIS

Yin [80] encouraged researchers to adopt four principles in order to produce an analysis of high quality:

- **Show that the analysis relied on all the relevant evidence**
  The analytic strategies, including the development of rival hypotheses, must exhaustively cover all key research questions and all the available data. Interpretations should account for all available evidence and leave no loose ends.
- **Include all major rival interpretations in the analysis**
  Review literature to identify and address all alternative explanation for findings. If the data is not exhaustive to discuss or address rival explanations, the researcher is required to review, appreciate the limitations of explanations and suggest opportunities for future research.
- **Address the most significant aspects of the case study**
  The essence of the findings which addresses the research problem has to be clearly communicated.
- **Use the researcher's prior, expert knowledge to further the analysis**
  The researcher should demonstrate awareness of current thinking, trends and discourses about the case study topic.

The tenets of these principles are comparable to the tactics provided by Miles and Huberman to guide conclusion drawing and verification. An extended summary of reliability and validity in qualitative research is presented in Appendix B from the works of Sørensen.

Argumentation: Writing and Presenting Arguments

DEFINING ARGUMENTS

Now that we have discussed how to analyze, the next step is how to write and present our arguments derived from the analysis. In this section we will discuss how to construct and present analytical explanations on the basis of qualitative data. While acknowledging that there are several approaches to argumentation, we draw on the guidelines presented by Mason [83].

Mason posits that making an argument is the construction of a perspective, an interpretation, or a line of analysis. It is a process in which the researcher is continually thinking about and engaging with those to whom the argument is being made as well as, establishing, the grounds on which they think the argument stands.

Arguments are "sets of ideas which are expressed and how they are constituted, in writing or in other forms, is fundamental" [83]. Researchers must show others what led them to suppose that their argument was appropriate or persuasive. The process involves working out how to construct, communicate, support and substantiate it.

TYPES OF ARGUMENTS

To argue convincingly, Mason notes that the researcher needs to understand [83]: what kinds of explanations or arguments can be built from the data; what kinds of explanations are outside the scope of the analysis; and what the researcher wants the explanation or argument to do? Based on these questions, four types of arguments are proposed:

- **Arguments about how something has developed:** Developmental arguments are used to explain how social phenomena, social relationships, social processes and so on have developed or come to be. It also describes a detailed, contextual and multilayered interpretation of the developmental processes.
- **Arguments about how something works or is constituted:** These arguments provide the 'mechanical' reasoning that explains how social

phenomena and processes operate or are constituted. This is because of the rich, contextual and 'local' nature of most qualitative investigation which is done in 'messy' contexts.

- **Arguments about how social phenomena compare: Comparative** arguments aim to draw some explanatory significance from a specified set of comparisons and therefore the logic of explanation is tied up with the mechanism of comparison. The focus of the context of data maximizes the chances of developing fully meaningful points of comparison.

- **Arguments about causation and prediction: Causality** is not about finding the cause and effect of a phenomenon in a straightforward fashion. It focuses on detail, complexity and contextuality which make a phenomenon act the way it does and not another way. **Prediction** is concerned with how and why social phenomena or processes happen in particular circumstances, and how particular ways can certainly support predictive ideas about how those things might vary in different contexts.

How to Argue

Arguing Evidentially
'I can make this argument because I can show you the relevant evidence'. The researcher has to clearly, logically and appropriately present the evidence for the argument (see Exhibit 48).

Exhibit 48 Example of Arguing Evidentially

In Case A, AA uses her phone's calendar functionality to schedule the times to supply her customers who need tomatoes. In Case B, customers are able to monitor delivery times of goods and plan for contingencies through text messages. This communication medium creates a borderless environment or redefines the "place" factor in transacting business with customers and creating more personalized services for them.

Personalized services lead to deepened relationships, which can contribute to customer loyalty and retention. Williamson (1981) refers to this phenomenon of "deepened relationships" as asset specificity, a transaction characteristic which depicts customers "locked into" a transaction for a considerable time. Source: [19]

Arguing Interpretively or Narratively
'I can make this argument because I can show you that my interpretation or my narrative is meaningful or reasonable'. If this is your argument, you will be concerned to show that your interpretation is sensitive, appropriately nuanced, and valid (see Exhibit 49).

Exhibit 49 Example of Arguing Interpretively or Narratively

Economic empowerment is evident in both case studies presented above. For example, Grace stated that: [. . .] I am able to send simple text messages to inform customers on maize prices and delivery times. AA also emphasized that: [. . .] Therefore, I do not need to be at the market every day, yet I still make my money. In this respect, the findings suggest that the women traders have gained some economic empowerment in improved income from cost reduction, decision making and control in managing the uncertainty in transactions with trading partners and customers. Thus, the transformational impact observed is the economic empowerment of the traders. Source: [19]

Arguing Reflexively or Multivocally
'I can make this argument because I can make you aware of a meaningful range of perspectives, experiences and standpoints, including my own'. The researcher has to show sensitivity to a range of interpretations and voices in the data, and willingness to critique and question the researcher's views, as well as those of others (see Exhibit 50).

Exhibit 50 An Example of Arguing Reflexively or Multivocally

Concerning the level of education and usage behavior, all respondents who had no formal education actively used mobile phones in all the stages of trading (see Figure 3). Noting that the number of respondents with no formal education constituted only 13 percent of the sample, **it is inconclusive to suggest a significant impact of education on mobile phone usage. However, the innovative use of calculators in trading was observed**. 12 out of the 18 traders (9 percent of total respondents) with no formal education claimed to use calculators in trading activities.

This ability to identify basic functions in mobile phones and integrate them in trading activities is arguably a function of some level of education and the perceived ease of using the mobile phones they owned. **On further enquiry,** these traders intimated that they often received help from their children, friends, relatives and sometimes customers in learning some of the functions of mobile phones, especially with "simple" text messages, calculators, and use of calendars as reminders. Source: [19]

Arguing Evocatively or Illustratively

'I can make this argument because I can evoke understanding or empathy in you, or because I can provide a meaningful illustration'. The researcher's aim is to get the readers to feel or understand experientially or by illustration whatever information is to be conveyed. Evocation can take text or non-text based forms (see Exhibit 51).

Exhibit 51 An Example of Arguing Evocatively or Illustratively

Second, the target market tends to be limited because of affordability and accessibility. The critical limiting factor on household access to the Internet is the investment involved. To set up household Internet access, it cost a total minimum of US$260 for a second-hand computer (with a modem) and one month household access.

At public access points, it costs an average of US$1.30 to browse for an hour in a cybercafé. With a daily minimum wage of US$2 (Mustapha, 2007), this means that Internet access is relatively expensive for a majority of Ghanaians and for businesses. Source: [72]

THEORY AND ARGUMENT

What is the relationship between theory and argument? As Coffey and Atkinson put it:

"Theories are not added only as a final gloss or justification; they are not thrown over the work as a final garnish. They are drawn on repeatedly as ideas are formulated, tried out, modified, rejected, or polished" [84].

To accomplish this, Mason explains that, researchers relate with theory in research in three forms of reasoning [83]:

- **Deductive Reasoning:** "Theory comes first, before empirical research and analysis, and is tested on or measured against data. The theory is not derived from data in this version…". The research will begin with hypotheses or propositions and the analytical task for the researcher is to measure or match up data against these hypotheses or propositions. It is like moving from the general to the particular – from the abstract/conceptual to the empirical.
- **Inductive Reasoning:** "Theory comes last and is developed from or through data generation and analysis". The researcher begins with the process of analysis whilst data generation is under way, and use theoretical sampling to augment this. Data is closely examined to identify explanations which appear to fit them. The researcher develops theoretical propositions or explanations out of the data, in a process which is like moving from the particular to the general.
- **Abductive (and Retroductive) Reasoning:** "Theory, data generation and data analysis are developed simultaneously in a dialectical process". The

researcher moves back and forth between data analysis and the process of explanation or theory construction. Coffey and Atkinson conceptualize the processes as abductive reasoning. The process is also comparable with Retroductive Reasoning which lies between deductive and inductive reasoning. Retroduction is "advancing from one thing (empirical observation of events) and arriving at something different (a conceptualization of transfactual conditions)" [85]. Transfactual conditions are conditions that exist for a social phenomenon to be what it is, and not something completely different. Retroduction enables the researcher to establish basic conditions or generative mechanisms for phenomena such as marketing capabilities to exist; hence without these conditions the phenomena will not exist [86]. Mason notes that in practice most researchers tend to draw on a combination of these approaches.

ARGUMENT AND GENERALIZATION

Generalization can be explained in two distinct ways [83]: empirical and theoretical generalization. Empirical Generalization is statistical in nature - based on a logic in which the researcher makes generalizations from an analysis of one empirical population (say, the sample, University of Ghana's students) to another, wider, population (say, all tertiary students in Ghana), on the basis that the study/ empirical population was statistically representative of that wider population. Theoretical Generalization – is not statistical but theoretical. The researcher needs to show that the explanation is being developed by trying out alternative explanations, and in particular by looking for negative instances. This type of generalization is more productive and appropriate for qualitative researchers. Hence, arguments are developed to generate theoretical generalizations. In the example below, a framework for examining the impact of mobiles on micro-trading has been developed. The research implications presented discuss the theoretical generalizations which stem from the proposed framework, related findings and propositions (see Exhibit 52).

EXHIBIT 52 AN EXAMPLE OF THEORETICAL GENERALIZATION

Concerning research implications, the conceptual framework, Figure 1, extends the knowledge on the application of transaction cost theory in information systems. Previous research has posited two key arguments (Waston *et al.*, 2005; Boudreau *et al.*, 2008). First, transaction cost theory tends to focus on the cost aspect of transactions whiles being silent on transaction benefits. The findings from this research explain how transaction benefits are influenced by the frequency of usage of mobile phones by actors in the transaction. The framework also explains how transaction benefits lead to incremental and transformational effects in the micro-trading activities.

Second, the transaction cost theory needs to be reexamined in the context of information economy where there is a dominance of electronic transactions and physical goods are increasingly becoming digital or virtual. This research, in response, explains how information systems, as in the form of mobile phones, influence the transaction characteristics such as uncertainty and frequency of transactions. Mobile phones enhance the timely communication of information in pre-, during and post-trading stages of micro-trading. Improving information exchange shrinks information asymmetry, reduces the demand uncertainty which underpins transactions, and increases the frequency of transactions between actors in the value chain (Jagun *et al.*, 2008). The study also explains how the knowledge of traders, trading partners and customers and dispersion of such knowledge between the actors influences the innovative use of mobile phones in micro-trading.

Hence, knowledge – intensity and dispersion – may be viewed as a transaction characteristic which can influence the achievement of transaction benefits. Discussions on knowledge as an additional transaction characteristic have earlier been conceptualized by Boudreau *et al.* (2008). This finding is welcome, since it adds to the three transaction characteristics – asset specificity, uncertainty and frequency of transactions – proposed by Williamson (1981).

COMPUTER-ASSISTED QUALITATIVE DATA ANALYSIS

A number of software packages have been developed to assist with qualitative data analysis. These packages can help qualitative researchers in a number of ways, namely:

- Storing and organizing data files and text
- Constructing and inputting data and diagrams from word processors;
- Creating an index system for data;
- Searching for words, phrases, or categories;
- Organizing data by categories or patterns; and producing counts of words and phrases.

These software packages are not a substitute for avoiding the close examination and re-examination of data and codes. They are not the solution to the detailed analytical and iterative processes as espoused by Miles and Huberman and also by Yin. The popular packages include: HyperRESEARCH, QSR NVivo, and ATLAS.ti. (A free trial version of HyperRESEARCH and tutorials can be downloaded from the ResearchWare site, at http://www.researchware.com) A brief comparison of the software packages written by Schutt [76] is presented in Exhibit 53:

EXHIBIT 53 EXTRACTS FROM SCHUTT ON COMPUTER-ASSISTED QUALITATIVE DATA ANALYSIS

Text preparation begins with typing or scanning text in a word processor or, with NVivo, directly into the program's rich text editor. NVivo will create or import a rich text file. HyperRESEARCH requires that your text be saved as a text file (as "ASCII"in most word processors) before you transfer it into the analysis program. HyperRESEARCH expects your text data to be stored in separate files corresponding to each unique case, such as an interview with one subject. These programs now allow multiple types of files, including pictures and videos as well as text. [350]

Analysis focuses on reviewing cases or text segments with similar codes and examining relationships among different codes. You may decide to combine codes into larger concepts. You may specify additional codes to capture more fully the variation among cases. You can test hypotheses about relationships among codes and develop more free-form models. You can specify combinations of codes that identify cases that you want to examine. [352]

Reports from each program can include text to illustrate the cases, codes, and relationships that you specify. You can also generate counts of code frequencies and then import these counts into a statistical program for quantitative analysis. However, the many types of analyzes and reports that can be developed with qualitative analysis software do not lessen the need for a careful evaluation of the quality of the data on which conclusions are based. [352]

In reality, using a qualitative data analysis computer program is not always as straightforward as it appears. [352]

Summary

In this chapter we covered a number of key issues concerning qualitative analysis. To begin, two types of qualitative data analysis approaches were discussed – the Miles and Huberman approach and Yin's approach. Beyond these approaches, we explained the concept of argumentation as espoused by Mason. The chapter is an introduction to these research activities; readers can refer to the authors discussed here to learn more through examples and further explanations.

In the next chapter we will discuss research proposal and research paper writing.

Chapter Discussions

QUESTION 1

Briefly explain the three components of the Miles and Huberman (1994) Data Analysis approach and use the components to assess any qualitative paper in your discipline vis-à-vis the analytical techniques used in the paper.

QUESTION 2

In relation to question 1, identify and discuss the types of argumentation used in the analysis section of the qualitative paper.

CHAPTER 8

Writing up Research

Objectives

This chapter seeks to explain the guidelines for writing a research proposal and research paper[9].

---

9 Picture source: http://differentiationstation.blogspot.com/2012/10/writing-process.html

Writing a Research Proposal

WHAT IS A RESEARCH PROPOSAL?

THE RESEARCH PROPOSAL plays a prime role in the pursuit of a graduate qualification. It is literally a written academic contract (not legal) between the researcher and the research supervisor, detailing what the researcher intends to study, how they intend to go about studying it, as well as how they plan on interpreting the results. Also, in itemizing what will be done in the research, the proposal gives the criteria for determining whether or not the particular research has already been done. It is important for the researcher to be clear on these things from the beginning of the research, in order to be able to complete the thesis or long essay on time. A weak research proposal will only lead to a long, painful, and often unsuccessful thesis writing exercise; which can be easily avoided.

By approving the proposal, the supervisor agrees in their opinion that the approach selected for the research is a reasonable one and is quite likely to yield the results anticipated. The researcher will then proceed to write the thesis or long essay. The proposal is not a fixed blueprint; hence, in writing the manuscript the researcher is expected to most likely discover things that were not anticipated in the proposal, but which need to be incorporated into the research. However, the minimum core intellectual contribution of the research is set by the academic contract (research proposal), which was agreed upon by both the researcher and the supervisor at the beginning of the research.

Characteristics of a Good Research Proposal

Exhibit 54 Outline of Research Proposal and Chapter One of Dissertation

RESEARCH PROPOSAL	CHAPTER ONE OUTLINE
INTRODUCTION • RESEARCH BACKGROUND • RESEARCH PROBLEM • RESEACH PURPOSE	RESEARCH BACKGROUND
RESEARCH OBJECTIVES	RESEARCH PROBLEM
RESEARCH QUESTIONS	RESEARCH PURPOSE
SIGNIFICANCE OF THE RESEARCH	RESEARCH OBJECTIVES
LITERATURE REVIEW	RESEARCH QUESTIONS
RESEARCH METHODOLOGY	PROPOSED RESEARCH METHODOLOGY
RESEARCH LIMITATIONS	SIGNIFICANCE OF THE RESEARCH
PROJECT SCHEDULE	RESEARCH LIMITATIONS
CHAPTER OUTLINE	CHAPTER OUTLINE
REFERENCES	REFERENCES

A good research proposal is pivoted on a good idea, with a basis in the academic literature. To achieve this, the researcher must live and breathe their topic, by spending time prior to the research reading, observing and conceptualizing material in the chosen area of interest. This should result in a discovery of the important dimensions of the topic, as well as areas in which a potential contribution can be made. A good research proposal often forms the foundation for Chapter one of the graduate thesis, with a few modifications as shown in Exhibit 54.

Some tertiary institutions have specific guidelines on how research proposals submitted to their outfit should be written. However, if the researcher is not given any guidelines on how to write the research proposal, the structure in Exhibit 54 can be adopted. The final draft of the research proposal must be well-presented and clearly written. A good title will clue the reader into the topic, but it cannot be used to tell the whole story. As a result, avoid complicated and long-winded titles. The introduction provides a better avenue to give more detail on the chosen title. Provide a good structure in the manuscript; use headings, be clear and straight to the point. Write short and precise sentences, and if possible insert images charts and diagrams to make your thoughts and ideas clearer. Remember to stick to the guidelines provided for the proposal and most importantly don't forget to keep to the submission deadline.

Components of a Research Proposal

INTRODUCTION

An introduction that is well-written serves as an efficient tool to capture the attention of the reader and set the context of your proposed research. It is pertinent for the researcher to get the reader's attention early on in the proposal. It is their only chance to demonstrate that the research is indeed novel and has the potential to bring something new to the existing body of literature. Hence, do no waste both your time and that of your reader with obvious and general statements. The proposal need not be worthy of a Nobel Prize; it only needs to be clear, straight to the point and based on sound reasoning.

Research Background

This section usually provides an introduction to the research issue. It may examine current discourse, trends or views concerning a particular social phenomenon in order to pose a research question. The research question will not be explicitly stated, but rather implied in an argument form (see Exhibit 55).

EXHIBIT 55 AN EXAMPLE OF A RESEARCH BACKGROUND

Topic: Social Networking at the Workplace – Prospects and Challenges
Social networking is increasingly becoming a phenomenon in the social and business lifestyles of employees. Statistics from the 2011 Forbes report on Social networking and business stated that 85 per cent of workers in America spend a minimum of 30 minutes of working hours to visit social networking websites (Forbes, 2011). These statistics are not too far from that of Africans, as a recent study in South Africa also found that 70 per cent of South African workers interviewed browsed Facebook during working hours (Ngu, 2011). Then again, beyond the concern of growth in the use of social networking platforms in the workplace, there have been concerns about the implications it has on both employers and employees (Jackson, 2012).

While some employers have been reported to be requesting access passwords to employee accounts (California Times, 2012); others are exploring policies and strategies to leverage social media in marketing and sales (Carmen, 2009; BBC, 2011).

Somehow businesses have to respond to this growing phenomenon. However, the questions are should employers be concerned - what are the potential risks and benefits of social networking in the workplace and how can businesses address these risks?

Research Problem

The research problem presents a situation in need of a solution, improvement, or alteration; or a discrepancy between the way things are and the way they ought to be (see Exhibit 56). It provides a rather general overview of the problem, with just enough information about the scope and purpose of the study to provide an initial understanding of the research. The research problem usually begins with a description of the problem from literature and practice, and ends with a research purpose (refer to Chapter 2 on identifying research gaps).

EXHIBIT 56 AN EXAMPLE OF A RESEARCH PROBLEM

Topic: Social Networking in the Public Sector in Mexico

The adoption of social media by the government confronts a series of barriers. Some of these barriers relate to records management, privacy and security issues, accuracy, and administration-specific requirements (Bertot *et al.*, 2012; Bryer and Zavattaro, 2011; Landsbergen, 2010 and Sherman, 2011).

As social media includes two-way communications, the risk of inserting malware into governments' websites exists (Bertot *et al.*, 2012), so the IT people should be prepared to protect government's information technology infrastructure.

Governments that would like to implement social media need to verify if people in charge of updating the media will have the time to update the new communication channel; they also need to answer other questions such as what to post, how and when often they will update (Bryer and Zavattaro, 2011 and Landsbergen, 2010). The lack of resources and procedures could undermine the accuracy of the information posted on social media.

Although the use of social media in Mexican state government portals is recent, the development of relationships between government and citizens is growing fast (Sandoval-Almazán et al., 2011). However, in contrast with other countries, to our knowledge, there is still no guideline for the use of social media in Mexico. The study of perceived risks, benefits, and strategies will be very helpful in the development of those guidelines.

Source: [20]

Research Purpose

The research purpose is a concise, clear statement of the specific goal or aim of the study. It usually comes as part of the research problem, and it includes the variables, population, and setting for a study.

The study seeks to explore the perceived risks and benefits of social media among public servants from Mexico, and especially the strategic elements to include social media in e-government policy and as a communication channel with citizens.

RESEARCH OBJECTIVES

Research objectives are specific, focused statements and questions that communicate in greater detail the nature of the study, as compared with the statement of the research problem.

The objectives of this study are:

1. To investigate the risks of using social media in the Mexican government.
2. To investigate the potential benefits of using social media in the Mexican government.
3. To investigate strategic guidelines for the use of social media in the Mexican government.

RESEARCH QUESTIONS

Research questions are **interrogative statements** that focus on **what variables** or **concepts** are to be described and **what relationships** might exist among them. Good research questions must satisfy a number of criteria. They must be as clear as possible to offer direction. They must be focused and appropriately complex, such that they are not answerable with a simple "yes" or "no" or by easily-found facts. They should, instead, require both research and analysis on the part of the researcher in order to be answered.

In relation to the above research objectives, the questions of this study are:

1. What are the risks of using social media in the Mexican government?
2. What are the potential benefits of using social media in the Mexican government?
3. What are the strategic guidelines for the use of social media in the Mexican government?

SIGNIFICANCE OF THE RESEARCH

This section discusses the potential benefits or implications of the research study on Future Research, Practice and Policy as shown below:

- **Implications to research**: how does it inform the research area?
- **Implications to Practice**: how does it inform managers, practitioners, employees, organizations etcetera.
- **Implications to Policy** (if applicable) - what do your findings tell government, the international community, development agencies etcetera.

In writing this section, the researcher must place themselves in the position of answering the question, "So what?" They must provide a persuasive rationale for why the study is important, to whom it is important, **and** what can happen to the field or society if the study is conducted or not (see Exhibit 57).

EXHIBIT 57 AN EXAMPLE OF SIGNIFICANCE OF RESEARCH

Topic: Electronic Banking in Rural Banks

The significance of the study can be viewed along three strands: research, practice and policy. Concerning the research significance, this study goes beyond current research on e-banking in rural banks by examining the strategies for implementing and integrating e-banking technologies. Literature on the strategic perspective of e-banking in rural banks is arguably non-existent in Ghana and perhaps this spreads to the West-African region.

Concerning significance to practice, the study will provide guidelines to other rural banks on the factors which influence e-banking adoption and strategic options to address challenges in managing and sustaining e-banking applications. This will be very helpful to ARB Apex Bank and to rural banks in its network.

Concerning significance to policy, the study will provide feedback on policies driving the computerization of rural banks which is critical to the operations of the financier, the Millennium Challenge Corporation, the government of Ghana and other donors who have an interest in supporting ICT integration in rural banks. These contributions to practice and policy will become necessary to the development of more advanced or complex functionalities for rural banks including internet banking and mobile banking.

LITERATURE REVIEW

The literature review section in a research proposal seeks to situate the research in the context of what is already known about a topic. The researcher is expected to show that they have a good knowledge of the body of literature, in which their chosen research area belongs and also have an awareness of the methodologies, theories and conflicting evidence in the chosen area. This should preferably be presented in a format that moves from the more general studies to the more focused studies. Research proposals have a limit on pages; hence the literature review need not be exhaustive. It will be more beneficial to focus on major research papers or public documents related to the field, and explain clearly how your research will make a contribution.

Literature review often seeks to explain the concepts behind the research and also present a theoretical approach to addressing the research questions. This is often difficult for new researchers as they may not be sure of the theoretical approach/model/factors to use for the research they are yet to begin. As a general rule of thumb, the researcher can use this section to introduce the relevant literature they need to read or review for the research. In addition they must explain the key concepts in the research, and the possible factors or issues to be explored. If a research framework has been identified the researcher can mention it. This is a good starting point. The researcher must aim at giving the reader enough ties to the literature such that they can appreciate the researcher's efforts at finding, reading, and understanding the literature in the field (see Exhibit 58).

Exhibit 58 An example of Significance of Research

Topic: Mobiles and Micro-trading Activities

This study investigates the impact of mobile phones on the micro-trading activities of women traders in Ghana. To obtain answers to this objective, four strands of literature will be reviewed. The first strand will explore the concept of trading/commerce from the perspective of the transaction cost theory. Transaction cost theory is arguably the most commonly used theory in studying issues relating to assessment of the impact of ICTs on commerce or trade (Pare, 2003). Transaction costs are described as "the costs of running a system" (Williamson, 1985: 19). The study will examine the costs involved in micro-trading and the impact of mobile phones on these costs. The second and third strands of literature will review literature on features of mobile phones and benefits of using mobile phones in reducing the costs of trading. The fourth strand of literature will examine the impact of mobile phones generated by virtue of the benefits. Mobile phones are conceptualized to have three effects on their adopters – incremental or amplification, transformational and production (Heeks and Jagun, 2007). These effects will be used to analyze the impact of mobile phones on trade.

Research Methodology

The research methodology provides an overview of the approach for the research. This section must clearly specify the manner in which the researcher intends to approach the research questions and the techniques that they will use to address them. One of the main reasons for including this section in the research proposal is to be able to detect any possible flaws in the research plan before they become serious problems in the research (see Exhibit 59). The research methodology:

1. Identifies the type of study to be carried out based on the following:
    *   Quantitative or Qualitative or Mixed Methods study
    *   Unit of Analysis: Individual/households, Organizations, Industry, Country

2. Outlines the research strategy that will be used to conduct the study and why those strategies will be selected. For example, Case study or Survey.

3. Indicates where data will be collected and what methods will be used for collection and Why.
   - This may include a description of the study population, the type of data that the researcher will be using for the research, and the data collection instruments to be used. For instance, Primary Data: Questionnaires, Interviews, Observation and Secondary Data: Industry reports, company documents.

4. Explains how the data collected will be analyzed
   - This should explain how the researcher will manipulate the data that they collect, in order to obtain the information required to answer their research questions. This may include either Quantitative data analysis techniques like Multiple Regression, or Qualitative data analysis techniques like the Miles and Huberman framework for Qualitative data analysis.

EXHIBIT 59 AN EXAMPLE OF A RESEARCH METHODOLOGY

Topic: Gender Differences in Electronic Banking Adoption

The study will use a quantitative approach to study the gender differences in the adoption of e-banking services among university students. The study's population is students in the University of Ghana Business School. A study by Turkson (2009) found that students enrolled in finance and accounting programs are more likely to adopt e-banking services. A survey will be carried out on a sample selected from students in the third and fourth year enrolled in finance or accounting programs.

A questionnaire concerning the adoption and use of e-banking services will be administered to 150 students. The study will also examine statistics on student banking activities from campus banks.

RESEARCH LIMITATIONS AND DELIMITATIONS

This section points out the constraints with regard to the research issues, which may influence the research. For instance, limitations related to Definitional concepts (what is included and what is not), Scope and Constraints (which respondents will not be involved and, perhaps why) and Variables (which data will not be collected/studied).

- **Limitations** are influences that the researcher cannot control. They are the shortcomings, conditions or influences that cannot be controlled by the researcher, that place restrictions on the methodology and conclusions. As part of the research proposal, any limitations that might influence the results should be mentioned. These limitations could be related to the analysis, the nature of self-reporting, the instruments utilized, the sample, and at times time constraints
- **Delimitations** are choices made by the researcher for the research, which should be mentioned. They describe the boundaries that the researcher has set for the study. The researcher must explain and justify the expected activities that are not going to be done. The researcher must also explain and justify the literature which will not be reviewed; the population which will not be studied; and the methodological procedures which will not be used. Researchers must limit their delimitations to the things that a reader might reasonably expect them to do, but that they, for clearly explained reasons, have decided not to do (see Exhibit 60).

EXHIBIT 60 AN EXAMPLE OF RESEARCH LIMITATIONS AND DELIMITATIONS

Topic: Electronic Banking in Rural Banks

A sample size of 50 computerized rural and community banks (RCBs) will be selected out of the 97 RCBs, based on proximity for ease of data collection and time constraint for the study. The study will not cover the use of electronic channels such as ATM, POS, mobile phone and internet since these channels have not yet been deployed to the banks. It will only focus on the computerization project under the mandate of the ARB Apex Bank.

There is also a possibility that some of the respondents may not return their questionnaires since it will touch on their financial and operational performance before and after computerization. The study will focus more on the banks than their customers in assessing the challenges and prospects of the project.

Project Schedule

The project schedule provides a synopsis of the main activities to be done in the research, using the chapter outline. It shows the time required to complete the research, as well as the time that it will be finished. The researcher must realistically assess how much time they have, including considering "No Show of Data", while writing this section. The project schedule must also be ideally presented in a diagrammatic/tabular form, so that it can be easily and clearly understood (see Exhibit 61).

Exhibit 61 An example of a Research Project Schedule

Chapter	Completion Date
Chapter 1	23rd May
• Meeting with supervisor	
Chapter 2	2nd June
• Meeting with supervisor	
• Revisions on previous chapters	
Chapter 3	5th July
• Meeting with supervisor	
• Revisions on previous chapters	
• Data Collection begins	
Chapter 4	6th August
• Meeting with supervisor	
• Revisions on previous chapters	
Chapter 5	30th August
• Meeting with supervisor	
• Revisions on previous chapters	

Chapter Outline

This section presents an outline of the thesis or long essay by detailing the objectives of each chapter. It also gives an overview of the number of chapters in the dissertation or long essay (see Exhibit 62).

Exhibit 62 An example of a Chapter Outline

Topic: Use of Technology by Healthcare Professionals

The first chapter comprises; research background, research problem, research purpose, objectives of the study, research questions, research significance, scope and limitations of the research and the chapter synopsis/organization of the research.

Chapter two focuses on a review of relevant literature on the overview of health information systems and the research framework. The third chapter entails the context of the study, which covers the brief overview of the health care system in Ghana and the profile of the case setting.

Chapter four deals with the methodological approaches which highlight the on study area, source and study population, sampling techniques and sample size, data collection instrument and method, data processing and mode of analysis, variables and ethical considerations. Chapter five entails data presentation, analysis, and discussion of findings. Finally, chapter six comprises the summary, conclusions and recommendations. The references and appendices follow this chapter.

References
See chapter on Literature Referencing

Research Proposal Outline with Word Count as a Guideline

1. **Cover page**
2. Each research report should be presented with a cover page which should state the title of the research and also outline the name and index numbers of the student(s).
   a. Table of Contents
   b. List of Figures (where necessary)
   c. List of Tables (where necessary)
   d. Abbreviations (where necessary)
   e. Definition of Terms (where necessary)
3. **Introduction**
   a. ***Research Background***   [maximum 700 words]
      - Usually provides an introduction to the research issue. It may examine current discourse, trends or views concerning social phenomena in order to pose a research question. The research question will not be explicitly stated but implied in an argument.
      - Provide a minimum of 15 references
      - Include some background statistics or an industry report or media report concerning the issue.
   b. ***Research Problem***   [minimum of 500 words]
      - A situation in need of a solution, improvement, or alteration; or a discrepancy between the way things are and the way they ought to be.
      - Provide a minimum of 15 references. At least 3 references should be on authors who support the need for your research or who have gaps in their research which you want to fill.
   c. ***Research Purpose***   [less than 100 words]
      - A purpose is a concise, clear statement of the specific goal or aim of the study.
4. **Research Objectives**
   - Provide <u>a maximum of 3 objectives</u>

5. **Research Questions**
   - Provide <u>a maximum of 3 questions</u>

6. **Literature Review** [minimum of 400 words]
   - Use this section to introduce the relevant literature you need to read or review for your research. Also explain the key concepts in the research and possible factors or issues to be explored. If a research framework has been identified you can mention it.
   - Provide a minimum of 10 references

7. **Proposed Research Methodology** [400 words]
   - Identify the type of study to be carried out. What research strategy will be used to conduct the study and why those strategies were selected? Where data will be collected and what methods will be used?

8. **Significance of the Research** [250 words]
   - Discuss the potential benefits or potential implications of this research study on Future Research, Practice and Policy.

9. **Research Limitations and Delimitations** [200 words]
   - Points out the limitations in the research issues, which may influence the research. Definitional concepts - what is included and what is not. Scope and Constraints - which respondents will not be involved and, perhaps. Variables - Which data will not be collected/studied?

10. **Project Schedule** [200 words]
    - Outline the schedule for your long essay or research activities. Be realistic and also add a timetable. You can use your chapter outline as a guide for the activities.

11. **Chapter Outline** [300 words]
    - Presents an outline for the long essay or thesis detailing the objectives of each chapter. Gives an indication on the number of chapters in the dissertation

12. **References**
    - Provide the references for all the journal articles and readings you referred to in the work.

Writing a Research Paper

In this section I attempt to provide a general outline which may be considered as being essential for a good research paper. Though this is not exhaustive, it will be of help, especially to young authors, in reducing the number of review cycles that submitted papers have to go through. The purpose is not to create a 'one best format', but to offer guidelines in the preparation of articles for submission to academic journals.

ABSTRACT

How do we write a good abstract? Emerald, the academic journal database (www. emeraldinsight.com), offers a set of guidelines for authors on how to write a good abstract. The guidelines advise that an abstract should summarize these key elements of the research paper or study (see Exhibit 63).

- **Purpose:** What are the reason(s) for writing the paper or the aims of the research? What concept do you want to present?
- **Design/methodology/approach:** How were the objectives achieved? Include the main method(s) used for the research. What is the approach to the topic and what are the theoretical or key arguments of your presentation?
- **Findings/Results/Observations:** What was found in the course of the work? This will refer to analysis, discussion, or results.
- **Research implications (if applicable):** What are the contributions to research? Which aspect of your work changes current research? What can researchers do with your research? What is new and how will that shape future research?
- **Practical and Policy implications:** What outcomes and implications for practice, policy, applications and consequences are identified? How will the research impact upon businesses or enterprises? How will it influence policy? What changes to practice/policy should be made as a result of this research? What is the commercial or economic impact? Not all papers will have practical implications.
- **Originality/value:** What is new in the paper? State the value of the paper and to whom.

Exhibit 63 Examples of Abstracts

Topic: Advancing E-commerce Beyond Readiness in a Developing Country: Experiences of Ghanaian Firms

This paper identifies factors affecting the assimilation of electronic commerce in Ghana and the solutions that Ghanaian firms have developed. Drawing from the elements of two electronic commerce readiness frameworks, the study analyzes the readiness of Ghana to support the conduct of electronic commerce at the firm-level. The study covers the government, technology, market and culture readiness factors. Findings suggest that social networks, managerial capabilities and government commitment have an attendant effect on the adoption and use of tangible resources like electronic commerce applications. The findings imply that future research and practitioner efforts should focus on developing a broader perspective to address electronic commerce challenges encompassing issues such as how firms can advance to more complex forms of e-commerce after initial e-commerce adoption.

Source: [72]

Structured Abstract

Topic: Mobiles and Micro-trading: Conceptualizing the Link

Purpose: This study investigates the impact of mobile phones on the micro-trading activities of traders in Ghana. The study develops a conceptual model analyzing the impact of mobile phones on pre-trade, during-trade and post-trade activities.

Methodology: A mixed methods approach consisting of a descriptive survey of 136 traders and a case study of two traders was adopted.

Findings: The findings suggest that traders primarily use mobile phones to monitor goods and pricing strategies, scheduling deliveries, and addressing inquiries and complaints in during-trade activities. Traders, including those with no formal education, also use the mobile phones as calculators in post-trade activities.

This innovative use of mobile phones is a function of their pre-knowledge which may have been developed through formal education and/or social networks. Improving information management through mobile phones directly or indirectly contributes to the economic empowerment of the trader.

Research Implications: The paper proposes a conceptual framework which extends the transaction cost theory to consider transaction benefits and effects in micro-trading. The study develops four propositions which can guide future research.

Practical Implications: The study provides practitioners with a 'theoretically-inspired' framework which goes beyond examining design and adoption, to identify needs and assess impact in mobiles for development initiatives.

Originality/Value: The conceptual framework extends work on the transaction cost theory in information systems and may inform future re-search in mobile phones and micro-trading activities. Source: [19]

INTRODUCTION

What is an introduction? In my research teaching seminars, I usually relate the intro-duction to "marriage introduction" done as part of marriage in African cultures. In essence, the family of the bride needs to learn about the groom and the groom or the man being introduced, has to be able to convince the family of the bride on why he is the best 'man' for their daughter. Similarly, in the research paper, the introduction sets the tone for the whole research paper. Why should the reader read the research paper? What are the theoretical and/or practical and policy motivations behind the research paper? The author has to:

- Introduce the topic/theme
- Highlight some of the research that has been done in the area of study (this should not be limited only to the country of study)
- Identify the gaps in previous research - areas that have not yet been addressed.

- Point out where your work is taking off from..., why your study is still important and what new knowledge it will add to the existing knowledge (see point 2).
- In the last paragraph state out: the main question or purpose of your paper and outline the structure of the paper.

LITERATURE REVIEW

You may use a relevant title instead of literature review. The literature review usually provides a detailed analysis of the research theme from the perspective of existing literature and further critiques and proposes perspectives or ways of addressing the research problem. The author is required to identify the following:

- Explain the concepts and issues
  - Discuss the main relevant arguments concerning the issues
  - Draw on existing and current research on the issues
  - Discuss their findings and how they help us better understand the issues
  - Review research in developing countries & Africa to highlight what has been done
- Understand how previous research was conducted: which frameworks and methods were used
- WHAT, WHY, HOW of the issue and WHERE you are going...Which gaps you need to cover

RESEARCH FRAMEWORK (IF APPLICABLE)

The research framework provides a theoretical lens through which the author seeks to address the research problem. It may provide a process or factor model which guides the investigative process of collecting data to answer the research questions. In some research papers, the research framework is developed or presented in the literature review. Others present it as an independent section or a sub-section of the research methodology. There is no wrong or right answer. The structure of the research paper and writing style of the author (logic and coherence of arguments) may determine the approach. The author is required to answer the following:

- How do we solve the problem
- How do we address the issue – which theory or conceptual framework do we use?
  - Develop hypotheses (Quantitative) or propositions (Qualitative) (if applicable)
  - A Concept or set of factors
  - A model of causal factors or interrelated factors
  - A set of propositions/hypotheses

Research Methodology

In this section the author explains the scientific methods used to collect data to answer the research questions. The author is required to:

- Identify and state their Research Paradigm (optional, rarely stated but may be deduced from the data collection process)
- What methods were used to conduct the study and why those methods were selected?
- In systematic fashion, the author needs to explain how data was collected (which has already begun excellently – just arrange it well)
  - Context – where are the study subjects located?
  - Unit of Analysis – What level of Analysis – Meta, Marco, Meso, Micro or individual
  - Data Collection Methods – Quantitative, Qualitative or Mixed Methods
- You need to explain in brief how you analyzed the data and dug out themes or answers or key lessons from your findings (see chapter 6 for examples).

Results or Findings

In this section the author presents the findings or results of the study. The author is required to:

- Use appropriate data analysis methods consistent to the data collection method. For example, in using a case study approach, quotes from your interviews should be evident and data should be triangulated from multiple respondents/interviewees.

- In a quantitative study, the appropriate statistical method has to be used and the choice of method should be justified.

DISCUSSION OR ANALYSIS

In this section the author analyzes the findings or results from the study. The analysis may require the triangulation of data from various research methods to create, explain or predict social phenomena. The author is required to state the following:

- What do the findings tell you about your research?
- How do the findings compare with previous studies highlighted in your literature review?
- Are there any contradictions with previous research?
- Why do these contradictions exist?
- What are the key and new lessons?
- How do the new lessons relate to the theoretical framework?

Use this exercise to identify parts of the literature review which are irrelevant to the study and thus need to be removed. Generally, literature that is not related to the discussion becomes irrelevant.

CONCLUSION

The conclusion covers three key sub-sections: summary of the paper and revisiting the research model/framework, research, practice and policy implications and future research directions. Some authors prefer to address these sub-sections as main sections. The author is required to identify:

- What is the 'takeaway'
  - Summarize in few words what the study did and what it has achieved.
  - Revisit the research model (this can be done in the discussion and analysis for a journal article, but for a long essay or dissertation, it can be done in the conclusion).
- Then discuss each of the following in a paragraph:
  - Implications to research: how does it inform the research area? This is an extension of the discussion on the research model.

- Implications to Practice (managers, practitioners, employees, organizations et cetera).
- Implications to Policy (if applicable) - what do your findings tell the organization, government, international community, development agencies etcetera.
- In relation to your findings, what should future research do?
    - Acknowledge the limitations of your research
    - Highlight what new or future research should do.
    - Suggestions could include using new methods or new units of analysis.
    - Suggestions should be relevant to your topic.

References
See chapter on Literature Referencing

Summary

Your work is going to be challenged, hence do not let the fear of other academics control your academic and professional career.

Though not exhaustive, in this chapter we attempted to offer elements of a good research proposal and paper, and outlined guidelines that can guide authors in future research. Read through your work - Presentation and Structure Counts.

Appendices

Appendix A: Brief Notes on Survey

SURVEY EXPLAINED

SURVEY SEEKS TO learn about a phenomenon in a large population by surveying a sample of the population. The two types of survey are: cross sectional survey and longitudinal survey (see Chapter 1). The survey method employs a variety of data collection methods such as face-to-face interviews, self-administered questionnaire, web surveys, and telephone interviews to record answers from a sample. These data collection methods vary in the potential outcome and resources needed [2]:

- Mail and Self-Administered Questionnaire
  - Relatively cheap, slow, lowest response rate
- Web Surveys
  - Cheapest, fastest, moderate response rate
- Telephone Interviews
  - Moderate cost, fast, moderate response rate
- Face-to-face Interviews
  - Expensive, slow, highest response rate

QUESTIONNAIRE DESIGN GUIDELINES

Crawford [87] proposes nine steps for developing a questionnaire, namely:

1. Decide the information required.
   a. What is the purpose of the questionnaire – research questions, research framework (constructs and propositions/hypotheses)?
   b. Which relevant literature underpins the constructs to be measured through the questionnaire?
2. Define the target respondents.
   a. Define population about which the study's findings will be generalized.
3. Choose the method(s) of reaching your target respondents.
   a. Define sampling procedures and data collection methods
4. Decide on question content.
   a. What phrases are going to be used to measure/collect data on the research questions and theoretical/conceptual constructs?

5. Develop the question wording.
   a. Are the questions' wordings asking what they are supposed to measure? Are there any biases?
6. Put questions into a meaningful order and format.
   a. What is the logical structure to be used – which question should precede another?
7. Check the length of the questionnaire.
   a. What is the average time for answering all the questions? Assess how much time is realistically available to each respondent to answer the questionnaire.
8. Pre-test the questionnaire.
   a. Pilot testing may be part of any, or all, of these stages of design. A pilot survey is generally a small-scale run-through of the survey and can also be used to check questionnaire coding and method of analysis.
9. Develop the final survey form.

FIVE POSSIBLE OBJECTIVES OF A QUESTION

a) To find if the respondent is aware of the issue
   - Do you know of any plans to build a school in this community?
b) To get general feelings on an issue
   - Do you think a school should be built?
   - A rating scale can be used for this type of question
c) To get answers on specific parts of the issue
   - Do you think a school will affect the local environment?
d) To get reasons for a respondent's views
   - Why are you against the motorway being built?
e) To find how strongly these views are held
   - How important is the tourist center that would be demolished, if the school is built?

Source: Curwin, J. and Slater, J. (2008) Quantitative Methods for Business Decisions, 6th Edition. Cengage Brain

QUESTION CODING

- Precoded questions give the respondent a series of possible answers from which one may be chosen or an alternative specified.
  - How many children do you have?
    - 0 1 2 3 4 5 6 7
- Sometimes codes are developed from the answers.
  - *Where do you live?*
- An open question will allow the respondent to say whatever he or she wishes:
  - *Why do you choose to live in Kumasi?*

Source: Curwin, J. and Slater, J. (2008) Quantitative Methods for Business Decisions, 6th Edition. Cengage Brain

QUESTION WORDING BIAS

- Two or more questions presented as one
  - *Do you use a Nokia because they are easy to **use** and **durable**?*
  - *YES/NO*
- Questions that contain difficult or unfamiliar words
  - *Where do you **usually** shop?*
  - How often is usual? Shopping also varies in terms of type of product, day of week and time of the year
- Questions which start with words meant to soften hardness or directness
  - *I hope you don't mind me asking this, but are you a virgin?*
  - *YES/NO*
- Questions which contain conditional or hypothetical clauses
  - *How do you think your life would change if you had nine children?*
  - This is a situation that few people will have considered....
- Questions which contain one or more instructions to respondents
  - *If you take your weekly income, after tax, and when you have made allowances for all of the regular bills, how much do you have left to spend or save?*

STRUCTURING A QUESTIONNAIRE

- **Field Notes**
  - Record Time, Date and Description of Natural Settings
- **Introduction of research**
  - Aimed at the interviewee
  - Definition of selected key terms (appendix or beginning)
- **Demographics**
  - Demographic data of respondent
  - Demographic data of the company/household
- **Main Questions**
  - Key sections may stem from themes/concepts/variables from the research framework
  - Key sections may stem from concepts/variables from the hypothesis
- **Other Questions**
  - Impromptu or emerging questions
  - Observations
- **Conclusion**
  - Review of answers, Future Review of transcription and Thanks

Appendix B: Glossary of "Validity and Reliability" Concepts in Qualitative Research

This glossary was compiled by Sørensen and is presented here only as a guide for readers.

RESEARCHER BIAS

One potential threat to validity in qualitative studies is "researcher bias" resulting from selective observations, selective recording of information, selective reporting of information, and allowing personal views to affect data interpretation. Strategies to enhance bias-free research include the following:

- **Reflexivity** - - means that the researcher actively engages in critical self-reflection about potential for bias (self-awareness and methods to control bias). Qualitative researchers often include a section in their reports that discusses researcher bias, sometimes called autobiography, in qualitative dissertations.

- **Researcher Journaling** - - the researcher documents his/her thinking during the research process.

DESCRIPTIVE VALIDITY

Factual accuracy of the account (Did what was reported as taking place actually happen? Did the researcher accurately report what was seen and heard?) Descriptive validity increases credibility and defensibility of research. Also adds to confirmability (ability of others to document findings). Strategies to enhance Descriptive Validity:

- **Investigator triangulation** - - use of multiple observers to record and describe the context and participant behavior and to interpret the data. Cross-checking among multiple observers helps ensure that investigators agree on what took place. Corroboration of observations across multiple investigators decreases chance of external reviewers questioning the research.

- **Audit trail** - - documentation and maintenance of records to allow others to verify the description. Also used for interpretive validity as researchers' thinking is documented, as is the process used to analyze data and create coding.

INTERPRETIVE VALIDITY

Accurately representing participant reality, accurately portraying the meaning attached by participants to what is being studied. The degree to which the researcher understands the participants' views, thoughts, feelings, intentions, experiences and portrays them in the research report. Strategies to enhance Interpretive Validity:

- **Participant Feedback/Member Checking** - sharing interpretations with the participants in order to clear up any misunderstandings. Asking participants whether they agree with what you have said about them.
- **Low Inference Descriptors/ "Thick, Rich Description"** - - Verbatim information, including the actual language, dialect, and personal meanings of the participants (e.g. direct quotations). Verbatim reporting allows the reader to experience the participants' perspectives.

THEORETICAL VALIDITY (PLAUSIBILITY)

This is the degree to which theoretical explanations developed from the research study fit the data collected. Theory refers to how and why a phenomenon operates/occurs and is more abstract than descriptions. It involves using theoretical constructs to explain findings. Strategies to enhance Theoretical Validity:

- **Extended Fieldwork/Long-term Observation** - - collecting data in the field over an extended period of time. This increases researcher's confidence in the patterns observed. More time in the field tends to increase the theoretical detail.
- **Theory Triangulation** - - the use of multiple theories and perspectives to interpret and explain data.
- **Interdisciplinary Triangulation** - - the use of other disciplines (art, sociology, history, dance, architecture, anthropology, etc.) to inform the research process and to understand the findings.

- **Pattern Matching** - - predicting a series of results that form a "pattern" and then determining the degree to which actual results fit the pattern.
- **Negative Case Sampling** - -intentionally searching for cases that do not fit your explanation so that you do not bias the data to support your theory. The final explanation should reflect the majority of the people in the study.
- **Peer Review** - - Discussion of interpretations and conclusions with other people, generally "disinterested peers" or other researchers not involved directly in the study. The peer plays the role of "devil's advocate", challenging the researcher to provide solid evidence for interpretations and conclusions. Discussions with peers who are familiar with the research can also provide useful insights.

INTERNAL VALIDITY (CREDIBILITY)

This is the degree to which a researcher is justified in concluding that an observed relationship is causal. Qualitative research is particularly useful in determining how phenomena operate (i.e. processes) and developing preliminary causal hypotheses and theories. Strategies for enhancing Internal Validity:

- **Researcher as Detective** - - Characterizes the qualitative researcher as he/she searches for evidence of cause and effect. The researcher carefully considers potential causes and effects by systematically eliminating "rival" explanations until the "case" is made "beyond a reasonable doubt." This may include the use of "hypothetical control groups" - - the researcher thinks about what would have happened if the causal factor had not occurred based on their own and others' expertise and published research studies. Generally, the researcher as detective makes a list of rival explanations (e.g. confounding extraneous variables) that are possible or plausible explanations for the relationship. The researcher must take the role of skeptic. Rival explanations are then checked against the data collected and/or sometimes require additional data collection.
- **Method Triangulation** - the researcher uses more than one method of research in a single study (e.g. survey, ethnography, experimental) or uses different types of data collection procedures (e.g. interviews, questionnaires,

observations, focus groups). The logic is to combine different methods that have different weaknesses and strengths.

- **Data Triangulation** - - the use of multiple data sources in a single study. This does not refer to multiple methods of data collection, but the use of multiple sources using the same method of collection (e.g. interviewing multiple students, observing multiple classrooms, etcetera). Data triangulation can involve collecting data at different times, in different places, or with different people. For example, if a researcher wanted to understand student apathy, data triangulation might include (a) interviewing parents, teachers, students identified as apathetic, and the students' peers) or (b) interviewing apathetic students in different class periods during the day and in different types of classes.

EXTERNAL VALIDITY (TRANSFERABILITY)

External validity is the extent to which you can generalize from the research to other people, settings, or times. Strategies to enhance External Validity:

- **Rich Context Description/Contextual Completeness** – the researcher should provide information on the number and kinds of people in the study, how they were selected, the nature of the relationship between the researcher and participants, a description of the context, information about informants who provided information, the methods of data collection used and the data analysis techniques used.
- **Replication Logic** - the more times a research finding is shown to be true with different sets of people or in different contexts, the more confidence one can place to generalize. This means repeating the study with a different group, or in a different setting.

EVIDENCE OF RELIABILITY IN QUALITATIVE STUDIES

- Researchers' methods are detailed, so that adequacy and logic can be determined
- Evidence of researcher qualifications is provided
- Researchers assumptions are made clear

- Research questions are stated
- Researchers were present in the context for an adequate period of time
- Data was collected from multiple sources
- Researchers saved data for re-analysis

EVIDENCE OF TRUSTWORTHINESS IN QUALITATIVE STUDIES

- Researcher acknowledges, shows sensitivity about, and maintains an ethical stance toward the participants.
- Researchers' work and analyses are fully documented, logic of data categorizations is evident, and relationships among concepts seem accurate within the identified theory.
- Descriptions are factual and provide evidence of minimal distortion due to omission or commission and include cases or situations that might challenge the conclusions.
- Data were collected from more than one source and there is evidence confirming the accuracy of the respondents' accounts.
- Researcher is tolerant of ambiguity, has searched for alternative explanations through multiple sources of data, and has devised ways to check the data quality.
- Evidence of formulating and reformulating interpretations and analyses of data including comparisons of data and checks of emerging hypotheses against new data.
- Researcher is self-analytical and recognizes limits of subjectivity; shows evidence of guarding against value judgments in analysis.
- Results are presented in a manner such that others might be able to use them
- Study is linked to a larger context
- Researcher acknowledges limitations of the study, as far as generalizing to other settings/contexts.

Appendix C: Philosophical Assumptions in Research

A paradigm is "a set of beliefs, values and techniques which is shared by members of a scientific community, and which acts as a guide or map, dictating the kinds of problems scientists should address and the types of explanations that are acceptable to them" [10]. Paradigms, as a set of beliefs, values and techniques, form the fundamental philosophical assumptions which define what 'valid' research is and the appropriate methods that can be applied in that research [11]. As various taxonomies exist to distinguish paradigms, there also exist various and diverse paradigms. The most commonly referred to or dominant paradigms that reflect the major theoretical directions in social science research are positivism, interpretivism, realism, relativism and critical realism [12,13,14,11,15,16]. Hence, research can be categorized according to these paradigms.

Each of these paradigms has its own set of epistemological, ontological and methodological assumptions that act as a structure to explain and differentiate them from each other [42]. Ontology in management research refers to how the researcher perceives the nature of social reality, whereas epistemology focuses on the study of knowledge and how it is acquired. It identifies beliefs about the acceptable and valid way to generate, understand and use knowledge. Methodology, on the other hand, refers to the framework used to conduct a research, within the context of a particular paradigm [70]. This can be contrasted from a research method which is independent from methodologies and paradigms [14]. It characterizes the set of specific tools and techniques used to gather and analyze the data as specified by the research methodology. Hence a research method, for instance an interview, can be used in different research methodologies. Ideally, a researcher will philosophically make inferences about what constitutes reality, how this reality can be known and the process of acquiring the knowledge. Thereby, the researcher will establish a distinctive logical relationship between the ontology, epistemology, and subsequently the methodology of their chosen research paradigm. Exhibit 64 outlines a summary of differences between the paradigms.

EXHIBIT 64 RESEARCH PARADIGMS

POSITIVISM

- ONTOLOGY (What is the nature of reality?)
  There is a single, objective and tangible reality.
- EPISTEMOLOGY (What is the nature of knowledge generated?)
  Value-Free. Knowledge generated is objective, free of time influences, and is context-independent.
- METHODOLOGY (How is knowledge created?)
  Researchers formulate research questions and hypotheses and then test them empirically under carefully controlled circumstances.
  Deductive reasoning
- *Examples of Studies in Marketing:* [88]

INTERPRETIVISM

- ONTOLOGY (What is the nature of reality?)
  Multiple realities exist, subject to human experiences and interpretation. Reality is socially constructed.
- EPISTEMOLOGY (What is the nature of knowledge generated?)
  Value-Laden. Knowledge generated is subjective, time-bound and context dependent.
- METHODOLOGY (How is knowledge created?)
  Knowledge is created through researchers identifying the various interpretations and constructions of reality that exist, and attempting to establish patterns.
  Inductive logic and emergent design
- *Examples of Studies in Marketing:* [89]

REALISM

- ONTOLOGY (What is the nature of reality?)
  Reality is "real"' but only imperfectly and probabilistically apprehensible, so triangulation from many sources is required to try to know it.
- EPISTEMOLOGY (What is the nature of knowledge generated?)
  Value-Cognizant/Value-aware. Findings are probably true...researcher needs to triangulate any perceptions collected.
- METHODOLOGY (How is knowledge created?)
  Social phenomenon is understood through hypotheses which are tested to establish patterns of associations and hence, the most possible explanation. Hypothetico-Deduction
- *Examples of Studies in Marketing:* [90]

RELATIVISM

- ONTOLOGY (What is the nature of reality?)
  Multiple realities exist. Reality as truth is not "absolute", it is relative, it is dependent upon 'something' and it does exist.
- EPISTEMOLOGY (What is the nature of knowledge generated?)
  The interpretation of the world requires some form of human processing
- METHODOLOGY (How is knowledge created?)
  The construction of knowledge is influenced by the worldview and research paradigm of a researcher. Researchers should focus more on creating and developing new 'useful' theories - useful solutions to specific problems.
- *Examples of Studies in Marketing:* [91]

CRITICAL REALISM

- <u>ONTOLOGY (What is the nature of reality?)</u>
  Two worlds – transitive and intransitive. Transitive is what we observe and learn with our mind - the perceptions of reality. Intransitive embodies the reality which is independent of what the mind thinks.
- <u>EPISTEMOLOGY (What is the nature of knowledge generated?)</u>
  Transitive world is value-laden and changing continually. Intransitive world has underlying structures and mechanisms that are 'relatively enduring' – that is what we want to study.
- <u>METHODOLOGY (How is knowledge created?)</u>
  Researchers seek to deconstruct and understand the structures and mechanisms underlying the subjective realities that exist. Triangulation from many sources is required to try to know it.
  Retroductive reasoning
- *Examples of Studies in Marketing:* [92]

An Example of a Research Proposal

User's Perceptions and Acceptance towards Enterprise Systems in Ghana

By Linos Lovelyn Anku

Practice Question: Identify the strengths and weakness of this research proposal

RESEARCH BACKGROUND

THE ALLURING CAPABILITIES of guaranteed high-quality performance, business performance and organizational performance of enterprise systems have enticed many organizations worldwide to initiate the integration of enterprise systems into their businesses (Kallunki, Laitinen & Silvola, 2011). This is a wave which propels the rapid changing nature of the world economy and provides solutions to the challenges of high competition organizations are responding to in order to support their business processes. This implies that the need of the time is to offer quality products and responsive services to customers and suppliers, and to add to customer lifetime value in order to gain competitive advantage. These demands are the fundamental alluring functions of enterprise systems. These systems include SAP, Oracle, PeopleSoft, Baan, JD Edwards, Microsoft, Sage, and Exact Software. Any of these systems integrates information and processes across organizational functional areas and levels, and empowers employees and supply chain partners to maintain and improve quality levels.

There is wide acceptance of these systems in both advanced countries (USA, UK, Indonesia) and developing countries (Kenya, Nigeria and South Africa), and various organizations have invested heavily and recorded major concrete and elusive improvements (Magni, Angst, & Agarwal, 2013; Didonet & Diaz, 2012; Dantes & Hasbuan, 2011;Yang, Stafford, & Gillenson, 2011; United Nations, 2014; Njiha, & Mwirigi, 2014; Ogunyemi & Olofinsao, 2014). For example, an empirical research specifically for Indonesian industries demonstrates that the implementation of enterprise systems acted to support organizations toward strategic and tactical impacts of businesses (Dantes & Hasbuan, 2011). Enterprise systems provide managers with model action environment for strategies, empower employees and supply-chain partners, and monitor quality by control plans in transactions. In the USA, enterprise systems implementation helps team network structure to improve customer satisfaction (Magni et al., 2013; Yang et al., 2011). In a developing country like Kenya, fifty-three percent of organizations, including the Commercial Banks, have adopted the implementation of enterprise systems (Njiha, & Mwirigi, 2014) and derives positive impact of data accuracy, communication and team works, and improved operations. In Nigeria, enterprise systems are used by the Insurance Companies to benefit from all the best-practices embedded in enterprise systems (Ogunyemi & Olofinsao, 2014).

Notwithstanding the benefits, organizations require a fundamental organizational change, and this makes the implementation very complex which may leads to substantial failures, sometimes (Ogunyemi & Olofinsao, 2014; Awolusi & Onigbinde, 2013; Lechesa, Seymour, & Schuler, 2012). For example, AB Plc, Insurance Company in Nigeria faced the challenges of lack of commitment and direction from executive management, inadequate training and education processes, indifference of employees, and reliance on external consultants which, if not because of the tenacity of owners, would dip the margins of the Company (Ogunyemi & Olofinsao, 2014). In South Africa, the main failure factors gathered from four enterprise systems-using industries were security and confidentiality (Lechesa et al., 2012). This implies that implementing quality enterprise systems do not necessarily give results unless the users see their usefulness. Reports on successful and failed enterprise systems implementations have led to propose and conduct an empirical research on user perception with the context of enterprise systems implementation.

Though there are indications that organizations have adopted and implemented enterprise systems to improve their performance in Ghana, extant literature is acutely lacking. This shows that over the years, there has not been any interest in this research area in Ghana.

RESEARCH PROBLEM

A review of extant research identifies a number of differences between this study and other studies. Fundamentally, all previous researchers have focused on other enterprise applications as though they are completely stand-alone from enterprise systems (Awolusi & Onigbinde, 2013; Lechesa et al., 2012; Kambarami, Mhlanga, & Chikowore, 2012; Ganesh & Mehta, 2010). Thus, enterprise systems publications are not in existence signifying that the academic interest in enterprise systems is driven by an interest in an empirical phenomenon rather than enterprise systems being a new research discipline (Schlichter & Kraemmergaard, 2010). In India, for example, a framework was developed to cover both the national and organization size aspects to identify and rank the critical success factors that influence the success of enterprise systems implementation at Indian SMEs (Ganesh & Mehta, 2010). Another classical example is recorded in South Africa where empirical studies are based on establishing the reasons for low adoption of enterprise systems in comparison with customer relations management (CRM) module in which the researchers conclude that the business environment is the key decider of adoption of enterprise systems (Lachesa et al., 2012).

In reviewing enterprise systems literature in more detail, it is found that the literature, first, is more oriented towards examining discriminating impacts between implementers and non-implementers (Magni et al., 2013; Didonet & Diaz, 2012; Dantes & Hasbuan, 2011; Yang et al., 2011; Morris & Venkatesh, 2010). For example, in Asia, the integration and collaboration of enterprise systems provide important benefits including added value, creation of efficiencies and client satisfaction to industries (Didonet & Diaz, 2012). Another instance is the implementation of enterprise systems in a telecommunications firm to moderate the relationships between skill variety, autonomy and feedback, and job satisfaction (Morris & Venkatesh, 2010).

Second, the studies echo substantial success and failure factors that need to be addressed (Ogunyemi & Olofinsao, 2014; Deng & Chi, 2013; Staehr, 2010; Ganesh & Mehta, 2010). In Australia for instance, top management support is identified as success factor in achieving business benefits from enterprise systems during the post-implementation period (Staehr, 2010). An example from India ranks the critical success factors as business plan and vision, top management commitment and support, project champion, focused performance measure, change management process, effective communication plan, risk management, post implementation evolution, quality improvement measures, selection of ERP package and organizational cultures (Ganesh & Mehta, 2010). And in Nigeria for instance, the most salient success and failure factors are concerned with the organization culture, training, project management, and involvement of regulatory authority (Ogunyemi & Olofinsao, 2014). All these studies consider the user involvement but rank it low.

Third, users' perception on system processes, user friendliness, quality and effectiveness of systems are important in successful implementation of enterprise systems (Garaca, 2011; Yang et al., 2011). While some researchers conclude that only perceived ease of use and perceived usefulness influence user satisfaction which has impact on usage (Garaca, 2011), others believe that social influence and cognitive instrumental processes impact on perceived ease of use and perceived usefulness before influencing attitude then behavioural intention (Shih & Huang, 2009; Liaw & Huang, 2013).

Fourth, different frameworks have been developed as effort to identify the factors affecting information systems success continued quickly in the nineteenth and twentieth century (Davis, 1989; Delone & McLean, 1992; Venkatesh, Morris, Davis & Davis, 2003). The Technology Acceptance Model was developed to verify low usage of installed information systems and concluded that computer systems cannot improve organizational performance if they are not used (Davis, Bagozzi, & Warshaw, 1989). Critical look at past research regarding TAM indicates that few studies have investigated enterprise systems user acceptance and usage, and only a small number of articles have been published.

While Davis (1989) proposed that the acceptance of technology is dependent on two main variables: perceived usefulness and perceived ease of use, DeLone & McLean (1992) proposed six distinct dimensions of information systems success: system quality, information quality, use, user satisfaction, individual impact, and organizational impact. Some of these variables are referred to as external influences (Davis et al., 1989).

The Unified Acceptance and Use of Technology was proposed and validated to give a unified theoretical basis to help research on information technology adoption and diffusion and suggested four variables: performance expectancy, effort expectancy, social influence, and facilitating conditions as direct determinants of IT behavioural intention and ultimately behaviour (Venkatesh et al., 2003). Meanwhile Davis (1989) identifies all these but nominates them differently.

These studies are both valuable and inspiring. Nevertheless, they are quite silent on the user perception in the context of Ghana. Thus, a study that offers such answer could provide great relieve, better understanding of issues and successful implementation of enterprise systems based on the relationships between perceived usefulness, perceived ease of use, and set of personal and organizational characteristics in the context of Ghana to help design interventional programmes for organizations. Also, a lack of attention to system and technological characteristics is a serious deficiency in most information systems research.

RESEARCH PURPOSE

The study seeks to evaluate the influence of perceived usefulness, perceived ease of use and set of personal and organizational characteristics on the acceptance and use of enterprise systems in Ghana. The implementation of enterprise systems at the service and production organizations requires evaluations to understand and establish the influence of user perception of enterprise systems in Ghana. The evaluation of the user perception contributes to the understanding of the factors affecting the adoption and implementation of these systems. The study further adds to the literature by presenting empirical data on modules of enterprise systems which stimulate users to implement them.

RESEARCH OBJECTIVES

The objectives of this study are:

(1) To explore the factors that impact attitudes towards Enterprise Systems usage in Ghana.

(2) To explore the moderating factors that affect attitudes towards enterprise systems usage in Ghana?

Research Questions

The research questions for this study are therefore stated as:

(1) What are the factors that impact attitude towards enterprise systems usage in Ghana?

(2) Which moderating factors that affect attitudes towards enterprise systems usage in Ghana?

Literature Review

The literature review focuses on the essential theoretical and practical knowledge within the area of enterprise systems (ES). It is important for researchers to be familiar with existing research prior to collecting their data to, first, serve as a guard against the risk of overload at the primary data collection stages, second, help maintain a sense of the topic's perspective and finally, raise opportunities for articulating a critical analysis of actual meaning of the data collected when the data analysis stages of the research were reached (Otieno, 2010). The specific areas covered here are concept of enterprise systems, modules of enterprise systems, characteristics of enterprise systems, critical success factors in enterprise systems implementation, commonly used enterprise systems and the business value of enterprise systems. Enterprise Systems refer to integrated and corporate-wide systems that automate core activities like manufacturing, human resources, finance and supply chain management to support the decision making process (Razmi, Sangari, & Ghodsi, 2009). These systems encompass different software components with an important characteristic of integrating information, departments, functions, and processes throughout the entire organization (Awolusi & Onigbende, 2013). It is also considered a set of packaged application software modules, within an integrated architecture, that can be used by organizations as their primary engine for integrating data, processes, and information technology, in real time, across internal and external value chains (Otieno, 2010).

Enterprise systems give business value, by increasing operational efficiency and by making available firm-wide information to help managers make better decisions (Laudon & Laudon, 2012), to the activities of the organizations. In this study, we will refer to business value as the organizational performance impacts at both the intermediate process level and organization-wide level, and comprises both efficiency impacts and competitive impacts (Rahrovani & Pinsonneault, 2012; Ramdani, 2012). These impacts are potential benefits which comprise flexibility, quality improvement, cost reduction, and productivity augmentation. Enterprise systems generic business values include managerial, organizational, strategic, operational related issues.

Concerning the theoretical framework, this study will use the Technology Acceptance Model. For almost four decades, many researchers (Garaca, 2011; Baker, Al-Gahtani, & Hubona, 2010; Davies *et al.*, 1989; Fishbein & Ajzen, 1975) have been studying events to determine how possibly an individual would decide to adapt to a new technology. Throughout these studies, the user perception of technology and its acceptance has been conducted in the information systems literature with Technology Acceptance Model (TAM). The TAM model is an expanded form of the TRA, and it proposes that anytime a user is faced with choosing new technology, such decision is influenced by how and when it will be used. The how and when is identified as Perceived Usefulness (PU) and Perceived Ease of Use (PEOU), the two representing the fundamental determinants of technology acceptance (Davies, 1989). Perceived Usefulness (PU) is the degree to which the individual believes that a new information system will improve their job performance. On the other hand, Perceived Ease of Use (PEOU) is the degree to which the individual believes that an information system will be used effortlessly and easily.

SIGNIFICANCE OF THE RESEARCH

The significance of this study can be looked along the following ways: research, practice and policy. In research significance, the study seeks to reveal the user perception of enterprise systems implementation in the service and production organizations in Ghana. This is significant because, very little literature exists concerning what makes users to implement enterprise systems as a whole on Ghanaian organizations, as well as the functional areas which impact the enterprise systems implementation in Ghana.

For practice significance, this study will provide detail guidelines to the organizations study and other similar organizations on what influence their employees to use enterprise systems and which modules of the enterprise systems are regarded most attractive to users. It will inform the organizations under study about what employees see in the systems they use so as to focus on them. It is important to indicate that the use of enterprise systems in many organizations has remain a key strategic resource, and to that extend, adopting and implementing enterprise systems means the focus of the organizations is towards achieving international standard.

Concerning policy significance, a feedback on policies to encourage competitiveness in organizations through the deployment of enterprise systems will be outlined. Many organizations in Ghana fail due to lack of guidelines to monitor and encourage competition, in the same way, no guidelines for adoption and implementation of these systems.

PROPOSED RESEARCH METHODOLOGY

The study will use a mixed-methods approach to explore users' acceptance and perception towards enterprise systems. The study population are employees of a financial institution, a tertiary education institution, and a processing company. A study conducted by Magni *et al.* (2013) tested hypotheses in a field study of 265 employees working in 44 teams in a large financial services institution. A case study will be conducted to document the context and profile of the organizations. A survey method will be adopted to allow forty (40) respondents to answer questions themselves. Besides the interviews, questionnaires and observations, secondary documentation comprising of reports and databases will also be considered. The appropriate data analysis techniques will be used to analyse the data collected.

RESEARCH SCOPE & LIMITATIONS

A sample size of forty (40) will be selected for ease of data collection and time constraint for the study. The study will not cover employees who do not have direct use of the systems except mangers of IT because effective cross-checking of information will be difficult to do. It will only focus on respondents currently in employment. Moreover, the researcher's choice of technology acceptance model (TAM) as a lens, will force the study to focus only on perceived ease of use, perceive usefulness, computer anxiety, and attitude towards use to the neglect of other factors in the findings that could provide interesting discussions. Nonetheless, the findings offer insight into enterprise systems modules and their influence attitudes towards use.

CHAPTER OUTLINE

The dissertation report progresses as follows; the first chapter provides a short introduction into the research area. In order to present a clear picture, the problem is discussed which leads to the research purpose, research objectives, research questions, research significance and, scope and limitation of research. The second chapter focuses on the essential theoretical knowledge within the area of enterprise systems comprising the characteristics, components, critical success factors, commonly used enterprise systems, user perception, and business values. Furthermore, a research framework which entails technology acceptance model (TAM) was discussed paving way for the establishment of a hypothetical research model.

In the third chapter, the context of the study is systematically presented, ranging from its establishment, through transformation phases, to the purpose for it establishment. The Chapter four deals with the findings of the study. These findings are the results of the data collected from the study area. The sampling techniques and sample size, data collection instrument and method, data processing and mode of analysis, variables and ethical considerations are also presented. Chapter five includes data presentation, analysis, and discussion of findings.

Finally, chapter six comprises the summary of the study in order to determine whether the research questions have been answered and in that way, fulfills the purpose of this study. This chapter will also give ideas for future research that appear throughout the writing process.

Common Errors in Submitted Dissertations

1. Clarity in thought of sentences
2. Using the same author – repeatedly in 50 – 150 words or consecutive sentences
3. Spelling mistakes
4. Missing full stops and Punctuations
5. Poor grammar
6. Poor structure
7. Possible Plagiarism
8. Referencing error – wrong positioning of brackets. Thus, …. "Johnson (2011)" at the end of a sentence is wrong. It should be …… "(Johnson, 2011)".
9. Reference Needed - Every 50 words should at least have a reference – especially if it is a key argument
10. Outdated references.….introduce more 2011, 2012, 2013, 2014, 2015 literature
11. Paragraphing – sentences combined and poor spacing
12. Poor in-text referencing. For example, no need for initials, poor placement of commas
13. Incomplete sections. Especially you need to end each chapter with a summary. You also need to know how to end sub-sections and link to the next sub-section.
14. Spacing needed between words
15. Too much extra spacing between words
16. Referencing error – no brackets, not using appropriate referencing style.
17. Using or repeating the same reference over and over again. Showing lack of extensive reading and over-reliance on one reference = not analytical
18. Poor link to the purpose of the research and refusal to make a definite statement as to what the position of the thesis or author of the thesis is??
19. Poor link between paragraphs. Hanging paragraphs – no link with previous paragraphs
20. Lacking clarity to the discussion in the section. Rephrase.
21. Remove the full stop before the reference

22. Split the sentence. Too long and confusing...

23. Remove commas before between Surname and brackets eg. Boateng, (2009) – remove comma

24. Abbreviation used without outlining the full phrase or collection of words. What does it stand and for?

25. Too much Descriptive writing

26. Using terminologies or concepts with little explanation or supporting discussion

27. Magical inferences – inferences based on nothing substantive and no references provided

28. Keep it simple – not needed. There is a need to provide a focus and scope for statements, questions and discussions.

29. Error in hypothesis formulation. E.g.: Mixing different level of analysis in research objectives/hypothesis

30. Putting relative measures which into hypothesis – like "higher" performance; "lower effort expectancy". You cannot measure higher or lower – unless a measurement is established from theory

31. Poor structure/the section is in the wrong place.

32. Missing sections: a quick jump to another section – hence some other sections should come before that section

33. Poor referencing of diagram/figures/tables. For example

34. Tables/Figures are put in the work but never mentioned in the discussion

35. Tables/Figures are wrongly referenced in discussion (say Figure 2) but on the actual exhibit, it is called Figure 4.

36. Provide illustrations, Figures, Tables or Diagrams to enhance understanding and explanation.

37. Incomplete reference

38. No definite statement or conclusion – something missing

39. Hypothesis is inconsistent with data analysis being used

40. Not required – Data analysis from poor conceptualization of research problem and objectives

41. Data analysis is flawed since there is error in sampling or data collection or data used in analysis

42. Purpose of study is not developed on substantial evidence or academic work
43. Title of section and content presented not linked
44. Incomplete table of contents
45. Writing in the future tense – like in a research proposal
46. Missing references

Practice Questions

QUESTION 1
Exhibit 1 Selling Used-Cars Online

Lankah Consult began in 2003 as a general merchant which sells used-cars to Ghanaians through the Internet. The cars are imported from Germany and United States of America (USA) and sold to customers through their website. The firm has no physical warehouse or showroom. The passage, below, captures activities conducted between the manager, John, and clients.

A majority of potential customers who made enquiries lost interest after realizing that the firm had no physical showroom. John had earlier anticipated this situation, and had shipped the first two cars to Ghana before advertising them. Due to the skepticism of customers, John focused on using social interaction to develop a personal business relationship with them. One of the customers, a resident medical doctor comments that,

> *"With the exception of the weekends, I barely had time to visit the cybercafé to check my emails during the week. John used to frequently meet up with me in the hospital during weekdays to discuss the options available and my preferences. This information was then relayed to Braun. By the weekend, I received details and pictures of my cars of interest through email. I download them and sometimes forward them to my fiancée. By the time I met John during the following week, I would have my questions and/or decision on the purchase."*

Though this was unsustainable for a large number of customers, John explains that it was necessary as the firm was just building its clientele and the Internet and telephone conversations were relatively not enough to do business within the Ghanaian culture.

Using the above passage, identify descriptive codes, topical codes and inferential/analytical codes, and draw two (2) selective conclusions.

QUESTION 2

In reference to a selected research topic of your choice, discuss an appropriate methodology for your research purpose and questions.

QUESTION 3

EXHIBIT 1: E-BANKING IN RURAL AND COMMUNITY BANKS (RCBs)

A sample size of 50 computerized RCBs will be selected out of the 97 based on proximity for ease of data collection and time constraint for the study. The study will not cover the use of electronic channels such as automated teller machines (ATMs), mobile phones and Internet since these channels have not yet been deployed to the banks. There is also a possibility that some of the respondents may not return their questionnaires since it will touch on their financial and operational performance before and after computerisation. The study will focus more on the banks than their customers in assessing the challenges and prospects of the project.

Briefly explain research limitations and delimitations and identify the limitations and delimitations in Exhibit 1.

QUESTION 4

In the 2014/15 first semester, a student submitted his long essay to his supervisor for review. An extract from the literature review states that,

> "The victims of sexual harassment suffer a range of consequences, from lowered self-esteem and loss of self-confidence to withdrawal from social interaction, changed career goals, and depression (Adams, Kottke, and Padgitt, 1983; Dziech and Weiner, 1990). For example, Adams et al. (1983) noted that 13 percent of women students said they avoided taking a class or working with certain professors because of the risk of harassment".

Based on your understanding literature review, evaluate the potential strengths and weaknesses of this extract.

QUESTION 5

Kwame Eshun purchased a newspaper, Weekly Times, on 3rd June 2014. Kwame read an article titled, 'Written Examinations Abolished in Kwahu University' and authored by Kwame's sister, Abena Andoh. The article was published on page 24 in the newspaper. Kwame intends to use the sister's article in his long essay; hence, briefly explain the relevance of literature referencing and develop the reference for the article using APA referencing style.

QUESTION 6

In reference to your term paper, briefly outline the sampling approach you used in collecting data for your case study. Discuss two (2) challenges you faced in collecting data and the measures you took to address them.

QUESTION 7

Briefly explain one theory or conceptual model that can be applied to carry out research by a student in the business school. Your answer should discuss the constructs, logic and assumptions/boundary conditions of the theory or conceptual model.

QUESTION 8

A student is conducting a research on social networking in the public sector. Briefly explain research gaps and using examples, discuss how the student can analytically review literature to establish a research gap and define a research purpose or focus.

QUESTION 9

In reference to your term paper, select a topic of your choice and develop the following:

- (a) Research Problem (give at least two references);
- (b) Research Purpose;
- (c) Research Objectives;
- (d) Research Questions.

QUESTION 10

Discuss the relationship between the Research Proposal and Chapter One of a long essay. Your answer should outline and briefly discuss each of the components of a research proposal.

QUESTION 11

In qualitative research, the researcher is advised to be aware of his/her own biases. Discuss the implications of this statement for someone conducting interviews in a research.

QUESTION 12

A student is conducting a research on the use of mobile phones by market women in Accra:

    a)   Using examples briefly identify and explain the following research terminologies in relation to the study: Survey, Study Location/Area, Study Population, Sample, Primary Data, and Secondary Data.

    b)   Supposing the student has a budget of GHS 1,000.00 (US$ 250), develop a research budget covering the relevant activities to carry out this research.

QUESTION 13

EXHIBIT 1: SOCIAL NETWORKING IN THE WORKPLACE

Social networking is increasingly becoming a phenomenon in the social and business lifestyles of employees. Statistics from the 2013 Forbes report on Social networking and business stated that, 85 per cent of workers in America spend a minimum of 30 minutes of working hours to visit social networking websites (Forbes, 2013). These statistics are not too far from that of Africans, as a recent study in Ghana also found that 70 per cent of Ghanaian workers interviewed browsed Facebook during working hours (Quaye, 2013).

Using the Exhibit 1, briefly explain literature review and discuss the phrase, *"Literature review is about argument, evidence and illustration"*.

QUESTION 14

Using relevant examples, explain the role of case studies in development finance research and outline the differences between single and multiple case studies in research.

Works Cited

[1]   L. Henrichsen, M. T. Smith, and D. S. Baker. (1997) BYU Department of Linguistics. [Online].   http://linguistics.byu.edu/faculty/henrichsenl/researchmethods/ RM_0_01.html

[2]   W. L. Neuman, *Basics of Social Research: Qualitative and Quantitative Approaches, 2 Edition*. Pearson Education, 2011.

[3]   D. Blankenship, *Applied Research and Evaluation Methods in Recreation*. Human Kinetics, 2010.

[4]   C. Cornell University Library. (2012, Mar.) The Seven Steps of the Research Process. [Online]. http://olinuris.library.cornell.edu/ref/research/skill1.htm

[5]   N. Alvin Sherman Libary. (2005) The Research Process. [Online]. http://www. nova.edu/library/dils/lessons/researchprocess/

[6]   J. Draper, "The relationship between research question and research design," in *Research into Practice: Essential Skills for Reading and Applying Reasearch in Nursing and Health Care*. Edinburgh: Bailliere Tindall, 2004, p. 69–84.

[7]   K. Parahoo, *Nursing research: principles, process and issues*. Basingstoke: Macmillan, 1997.

[8]   D. M. Mertens, *Research methods in Education and Psychology: Integrating diversity with quantitative and qualitative approaches*. Sage Publications, Inc, 1998.

[9]   D. M. Ha, "Analyses of the prevailing research paradigms in education," *Journal of Science and Technology, Dai Hoc Da Nang*, vol. 4, no. 45, pp. 189-198, 2011.

[10]   T. Kuhn, *The Structure of Scientific Revolutions*. Chicago: University of Chicago Press, 1970.

[11]   M. D. Myers and D. Avison, "An Introduction to Qualitative Research in Information Systems," in *Qualitative Research in Information Systems, A Reader*. London: Sage Publications, 2002, pp. 3-12.

[12]   W. J. Orlikowski and J. J. Baroudi, "Studying Information Technology in Organisations: Research Approaches and Assumptions," *Accounting, Management And Information Technologies*, vol. 1, no. 1, pp. 9-42, 1991.

[13]   J. J. Baroudi, "Studying Information Technology in Organisations: Research Approaches and Assumptions," *Information Systems Research*, vol. 2, no. 1, pp. 1-28, 1991.

[14]   S. Sarantakos, *Social Research, Second Edition*. Basingstoke, Hampshire: Palgrave, 1998.

[15]   P. J. Dobson, "Critical Realism and Information Systems Research: Why Bother with Philosophy," *Information Research*, vol. 7, no. 2, pp. 1-13, 2002.

[16]   S. Kim, "Research Paradigms in Organisational Learning and Performance: Competing Modes of Inquiry," *Information Technology, Learning, and Performance Journal,*, vol. 21, no. 1, pp. 9-18, 2003.

[17]   V. Jupp, "Time Series Design," in *The SAGE Dictionary of Social Research Methods*. Sage Publications, 2006.

[18]   J. Abor, "Corporate governance and financing decisions of Ghanaian listed firms," *Corporate Governance*, vol. 7, no. 1, pp. 83-92, 2007.

[19]   R. Boateng, "Mobile Phones and Micro-Trading Activities – Conceptualizing The Link," *Info: The Journal for Policy, Regulation and Strategy*, vol. 13, no. 5, pp. 48-62, 2011.

[20]   S. Picazo-Vela, I. Gutiérrez-Martínez, and L. F. Luna-Reye, "Understanding risks, benefits, and strategic alternatives of social media applications in the public sector," *Government Information Quarterly*, vol. 29, no. 4, pp. 504-511, 2012.

[21]   E. Collins. (2000, Mar.) Research Gaps Academic Writer 2000. [Online]. http://vlc.polyu.edu.hk/academicwriter/Evidence/Secondary%20Sources/researchgaps.htm,

[22]   R. Boateng, *When the lights go out... A Resource-Based Theory Analysis of E-commerce in Developing Countries: The Case of Ghanaian Firms*, Ghana: PearlRichards Foundation and Craft Concepts. Accra, Ghana: PearlRichards Foundation, 2011.

[23]   E. Asiedu, I. Kalonda-Kanyama, L. Ndikumana, and A. Nti-Addae, "Access to Credit by Firms in Sub-Saharan Africa: How Relevant is Gender?," *American Economic Review: Papers & Proceedings 2013*, vol. 103, no. 3, p. 293–297, 2013.

[24] O. Olivares. (2004) Social Sciences Team Librarian, University of Arizona Libraries. [Online]. http://www.library.arizona.edu/tutorials/litreviews/

[25] Merriam-Webster. (2014) Merriam-Webster. [Online]. http://www.merriam-webster.com/dictionary/synthesis

[26] U. o. Queensland. (2012) University of Queensland. [Online]. http://www.uq.edu.au/student-services/phdwriting/phfaq23.html

[27] Emerald Group Publishing Limited. (2012) Emerald Group Publishing Limited. [Online]. http://www.emeraldinsight.com/authors/guides/write/literature.htm?part=1

[28] D. Taylor. (2013) Universtiy of Toronto. [Online]. http://www.writing.utoronto.ca/advice/specific-types-of-writing/literature-review

[29] U. o. Reading. (2014, Jan.) Study Advice. [Online]. http://www.reading.ac.uk/internal/studyadvice/StudyResources/Reading/sta-effective.aspx

[30] R. Boateng, A. Molla, and R. Heeks, "E-commerce in Developing Economies: A Review of Theoretical Frameworks and Approaches," in *Emerging Markets and E-commerce in Developing Economies*. Hershey, PA: IGI Publishing, 2009.

[31] R. Boateng, R. Hinson, R. Heeks, and M. A., "Ecommerce in LDCs: Summary Evidence and Implications," *Journal of African Business*, vol. 9, no. 2, pp. 257-285.

[32] W. G. Zikmund, *Business Research Methods, 7th edition*. Thomson/South-Western, 2003.

[33] C. Fisher, *Researching and Writing a Dissertation, An Essential Guide For Business Students*. Essex: Pearson Education Limited, 2010.

[34] R. Duncombe and R. Boateng, "Mobile Phones and Financial Services in Developing Countries: A Review of Concepts, Methods, Issues, Evidence and Future Research Directions," *Third World Quarterly*, vol. 30, no. 7, p. 1237–1258, 2009.

[35] R. Heeks, "Theorizing ICT4D Research," *Information and Communication Technologies and International Development (Special Issue)*, vol. 3, no. 3, pp. 1-4, 2006.

[36] Henning, T.B. (2011, Feb.) University Writing Centre, School of Liberal Arts, Indiana University. [Online]. http://liberalarts.iupui.edu/uwc/

[37] T. W. Centre. (2013) The Writing Centre, University of North Carolina at Chapel Hill. [Online]. https://writingcenter.unc.edu/handouts/literature-reviews/

[38]   HowtoGeek.com. (2013, Nov.) How to geek. [Online]. http://www.howtogeek.
       com/54891/using-microsoft-word-2010s-references-feature-for-students/

[39]   S. B. Bacharach, "Organizational Theories: Some Criteria for Evaluation,"
       Academy of Management Review, pp. 496-515, 1989.

[40]   A. Bhattacherjee, *Social Science Research: Principles, Methods, and Practices*.
       Florida: Global Text Project, 2012.

[41]   S. Gregor, "The nature of theory in information systems," *MIS Quarterly*, vol. 30,
       no. 3, pp. 611-642, 2006.

[42]   J. W. Creswell, *Qualitative Inquiry and Research Design: Choosing Among Five
       Approaches*. Sage Publications, Inc., 2007.

[43]   N. R. Council, *Food Marketing to Children and Youth - Threat or Opportunity?*,
       *Committee on Food Marketing and the Diets of Children and Youth, Food and
       Nutrition Board*. Washington, DC: The National Academies Press, 2006.

[44]   F. D. Davis, *A Technology Acceptance Model for Empirically Testing New End-User
       Information Systems: Theory and Results, Doctoral Dissertation*. Cambridge,
       MA: MIT Sloan School of Managemen, 1985.

[45]   S. Reeves, M. Albert, A. Kuper, and B. H. Hodges, "Why Use theories in Qualitative
       Research," *BMJ*, p. 337, 2008, doi:10.1136/bmj.a949.

[46]   I. Ajzen and M. Fishbein, *Understanding Attitudes and Predicting Social
       Behaviour*. Englewood Cliffs, NJ: Prentice Hall, 1980.

[47]   E. Overby, "Process Virtualisation Theory and the Impact of Information
       Technology," *Organisation Science*, vol. 19, no. 2, p. 277–291, 2008.

[48]   M. B. Miles and A. M. Huberman, *An expanded sourcebook qualitative data
       analysis*. Sage, 1994.

[49]   C. Robson, *Real world research: a resource for users of social research methods in
       applied settings*. Chichester: Wiley, 2011.

[50]   N. K. Denzin and Y. S. Lincoln, *Handbook of qualitative research*. Thousand
       Oaks: Sage Publications, 1994.

[51]   M. Q. Patton, *Qualitative Research and Evaluation Methods, Third Edition*.
       Thousand Oaks: Sage Publications, Inc., 2002.

[52]   N. Mack, C. Woodsong, K. M. MacQueen, G. Guest, and E. Namey, *Qualitative
       Research Methods: A Data Collector's Field Guide*. North Carolina: Family Health
       International, 2005.

[53] U. Flick, *An Introduction to Qualitative Research – Fourth Edition*. London: Sage, 2009.

[54] J. W. Creswell, *Qualitative inquiry and research design: Choosing among the five traditions (3rd ed.)*. Thousand Oaks: Sage, 2012.

[55] B. Johnson and L. Christensen, *Educational research: Quantitative, qualitative, and mixed approaches. 3rd Edition*. Thousand Oaks, CA: Sage Publication, 2008.

[56] S. B. Merriam and Associates, *Qualitative research in practice. Examples for discussion and analysis*. San Francisco: Jossey Bass, 2002.

[57] V. E. Worthen and B. W. McNeill, "A phenomenological investigation of good supervision events," *Journal of Counselling Psychology*, vol. 43, pp. 25-34, 1996.

[58] P. T. Whitfield and B. J. Klug, "From aspirant to professional: The transformation of American Indians who would be teachers. Results of a five-year ethnographic study," in *Paper presented at the Annual Meeting of the American Educational Research Association*, New Orleans, LA, April, pp. 24-28.

[59] N. J. Smith-Sebasto and L. M. Walker, "Toward a grounded theory for residential environmental education: A case study of the New Jersey School for Conservation," *Journal of Environmental Education*, vol. 37, no. 1, pp. 37-42, 2005.

[60] R. K. Yin, *Case Study Research, Design Methods, 2nd Edition*. Newbury Park: Sage Publications, 1994.

[61] I. Benbasat, D. K. Goldstein, and M. Mead, "The Case Research Strategy in Studies of Information Systems," *MIS Quarterly*, vol. 11, no. 3, pp. 369-386, 1987.

[62] C. Hakim, *Research Design: Strategies and Choices in the Design of Social Research*. London: Allen and Unwin, 1987.

[63] D. De Vaus, *Research Design in Social Research*. London: Sage Publications, 2001.

[64] N. Denzin, *The research act*. Englewood Cliffs, NJ: Prentice Hall, 1984.

[65] R. E. Stake, *The Art of Case Study Research*. Thousand Oaks, CA: Sage Publications Inc., 1995.

[66] G. Walsham, *Interpreting Information Systems in Organisations*, . Chichester: Wiley, 1993.

[67] B. Kaplan and J. A. Maxwell, "Qualitative Research Methods for Evaluating Computer Information Systems," in *Evaluating Health Care Information Systems: Methods and Applications*. Thousand Oaks, CA: Sage, 1994, pp. 45-68.

[68]   W. Tellis, "Application of a Case Study Methodology," *The Qualitative Report*, vol. 3, no. 3, 1997.

[69]   C. Sørensen. (2000) Qualitative Research Defined. [Online]. http://www.cedu. niu.edu/~Sørensen/502/powerpoint/topicD/qlnotes.htm

[70]   D. Wahyuni, "The research design maze: understanding paradigms, cases, methods and methodologies," *Journal of Applied Management Accounting Research*, vol. 10, no. 1, pp. 69-80, 2012.

[71]   J. W. Creswell, *Research Design - Qualitative, Quantitative and Mixed Methods Approaches - Third Edition*. Thousand Oaks: Sage Publications, 2009.

[72]   R. Boateng, A. Molla, R. Heeks, and R. Hinson, "Advancing E-commerce Beyond Readiness in a Developing Economy: Experiences of Ghanaian Firms," *Journal of Electronic Commerce in Organizations*, vol. 9, no. 1, pp. 1-16, 2011.

[73]   M. N. Abdulai, *Perceived Knowledge, Skills and Attitude (KSA) of Health Care Professionals towards Health Information Systems in Ghana: The Case of University of Cape Coast Hospital, MBA Dissertation*. Accra: University of Ghana Business School, 2012.

[74]   M. B. Miles, A. M. Huberman, and J. Saldana, *Qualitative Data Analysis: A Methods Sourcebook - 3rd edition*. Thousand Oaks: Sage, 2013.

[75]   R. K. Yin, *Case Study Research: Design and Methods (3rd edition, Volume 5)*. London: Sage Publications, 2003.

[76]   R. K. Schutt, *Investigating the Social World The Process and Practice Research 7th Edition*. Thousand Oaks: Sage Publications, 2012.

[77]   L. Richards, *Handling Qualitative Data: A Practical Guide*. Thousand Oaks: Sage, 2005.

[78]   K. F. Punch, *Introduction to Research Methods in Education*. Thousand Oaks: Sage Publications, 2009.

[79]   A. Edwards and J. Skinner, *Qualitative Research in Sport Management*. Oxford: Butterworth-Heinemann-Elsevier, 2009.

[80]   R. K. Yin, *Case Study Research Design and Methods Fifth Edition*. Thousand Oaks: Sage Publications, 2014.

[81]   R. Boateng, R. Hinson, R. Galadima, and O. L., "Preliminary Insights into the Influence of Mobile Phone in Micro-Trading Activities of Market Women in Nigeria," *Information Development*, vol. 30, no. 1, pp. 32-50, 2014.

[82] W. Trochim, "Outcome pattern matching and program theory," *Evaluation and Program Planning*, vol. 12, no. 4, p. 355, 1989.

[83] J. Mason, *Qualitative Researching, 2nd edition*. Thousand Oaks: Sage, 2002.

[84] A. Coffey and P. Atkinson, *Narratives and stories. In Making sense of qualitative data: Complementary research strategies*. Thousand Oaks: Sage Publications, 1996.

[85] B. Danermark, M. Ekstrom, L. Jakobsen, and J. C. Karlsson, *Explaining Society, Critical Realism in the Social Sciences*. London: Routledge Publishing, 2002.

[86] P. Downward and A. Mearman, "Retroduction as Mixed-Methods Triangulation in Economic Research: Reorienting Economics into Social Science," *Cambridge Journal of Economics*, vol. 31, no. 1, p. 77–99, 2007.

[87] I. Crawford, *Marketing Research and Information Systems. (Marketing and Agribusiness Texts - 4)*. Rome: Food and Agricultural Organization of the UN, 1997.

[88] M. B. Beverland and A. Lindgreen, "What makes a good case study? A positivist review of qualitative case research published in International Marketing Management, 1971-2006," *Industrial Marketing Management*, vol. 39, no. 1, pp. 56-63, 2010.

[89] D. H. Jernigan, "The extent of global alcohol marketing and its impact on youth," *Contemporary Drug Problems,*, vol. 37, no. 1, pp. 57-89, 2010.

[90] D. Bickerton, "Corporate reputation versus corporate branding: the realist debate," *Corporate Communications: An International Journal*, vol. 5, no. 1, pp. 42-48, 2000.

[91] P. F. (. Anderson, "On Method in Consumer Research: A Critical Relativist Perspective," *Journal of Consumer Research*, vol. 13, no. 2, pp. 155-173.

[92] P. Downward and A. Mearman, "On tourism and hospitality management research: a critical realist proposal," *Tourism and Hospitality Planning & Development*, vol. 1, no. 2, pp. 107-122, 2004.

[93] L. S. Cohen. (2009, Sep.) Mashable Social Media. [Online]. http://mashable.com/2009/09/11/banks-social-media/

[94] Fidelity Bank Ghana. (2012, Jan.) Twitter. [Online]. https://twitter.com/fidelitybankgh

[95] M. G. Durkin and B. Howcroft, "Relationship marketing in the banking sector: the impact of new technologies," vol. 21, no. 1, pp. 61-71, 2003.

[96] Central Queensland University Library. (2000) Central Queensland University Library. [Online]. http://www.library.cqu.edu.au/litreview/pages

[97] N. Dixon, *Common Knowledge: How Companies Thrive By Sharing What They Know*. Boston: Harvard University Press, 2000.

[98] A. H. Maslow, "A Theory of Human Motivation," *Psychological Review*, vol. 50, pp. 370-396, 1943.

[99] S. M. Ravitch and M. Riggan, *Reason & rigor: How conceptual frameworks guide research*. Sage, 2011.

[100] L. Kakkori, "Hermeneutics and Phenomenology Problems When Applying Hermeneutic Phenomenological Method in Educational Qualitative Research," *Paideusis*, vol. 18, no. 2, pp. 19-27, 2009.

[101] R. Heeks, *Implementing and Managing eGovernment: an International Text*. London: Sage, 2006.

Author Profile

PROF. RICHARD BOATENG is a technology researcher who focuses on developing, promoting and protecting ideas and concepts into sustainable projects of commercial value and development impact. Richard is an Associate Professor in information systems at the University of Ghana Business School. Richard serves as the Head of the Department of Operations and Management Information Systems at the business School.

Richard is also the associate editor of the Information Technologies & International Development Journal and serve on the editorial board of the Information Development Journal. His research experience covers e-learning, information and communication technologies (ICT) for development, electronic governance, social media, electronic business, gender and technology, mobile commerce, and mobile health at the national, industrial, organisational and community levels.

His research work contributes to the over 30 publications he has published on ICT adoption and usage in developing country contexts. He also has expertise in policy development and led a team to develop the University of Ghana guidelines for industry engagement and technology commercialisation. Since joining the University of Ghana in 2010, Richard has collaborated with other faculty to obtain not less than 1.2 million USD in research and project funds. These research and project funds have been obtained from organisations including Vodafone Group (global), Danish International Development Agency (DANIDA), International Development Research Centre (Canada), and the World Bank. Richard has also consulted for the United Nations Development Programme (UNDP), Ghana and United Nations Educational, Scientific and Cultural Organisation (UNESCO) Accra Cluster Office on technology and communication development projects.

Richard Boateng

Richard has a doctorate degree in Development Informatics and a master's degree in Management and Information Systems from the University of Manchester, UK. He is a British Chevening Award Scholar and a Dorothy Hodgkin Postgraduate Award Scholar. In March 2011, Richard received the Southern University (USA) Research Leadership Award, for contribution to ICT Research in Africa, awarded at the 4th International Conference on ICT for Africa, 26 March, 2011, held at Covenant University, Ota, Nigeria. Richard can be reached by richard@pearlrichards.org. His recent Global Report on Inequalities and Access to Communication can be accessed at http://goo.gl/IgzVB4

Index

L

Literature Referencing. 91
    APA Referencing Style 92
Literature Review
    Analyzing and Writing. 76
    Categorizing Literature 57
    Defined 37
    Harvard Rules 94
    Locate Literature 43
    Prioritizing Information Sources. .51
    Relevance 51
    Steps. 43
    Structuring Literature Review 84
    Summarizing an Article. 53

M

Mixed Methods Research 11, 157

P

Philosophical Assumptions 235

Q

Qualitative Data Analysis
    Computer-Assisted 194
Qualitative Data Analysis
    Argumentation. 187
    Coding. 175
    Data Condensation. 172

    Data Display. 172
    Memoing 177
    Miles and Huberman Data
    Analysis Approach. 172
    Quality. 186
    Yin's Data Analysis Approach . . .183
Qualitative Research 135
    Case study 146
    Enthnography. 142
    Forms of Data 149
    Grounded Theory 143
    Key Features. 137
    Phenomenology. 141
    Types 140
Quantitative Research. 10

R

Research
    Types of Research. 8
Research
    Absence of Research. 3
    Defined 2
    Goals/Purpose. 2
    Significance 4
Research
    Goal/Purpose. 9

Research
Time Dimension. 11
Research Gaps
Definition 20
Identifying Gaps. 28
Types of Gaps 20
Research Paradigms
Comparison and Examples. 235
Research Philosophies 235
Research Process. 5
Difference from Research
Design 6
Research Activities. 7
Research Topic. 15
How to Select 18

T
Theory in Research
Attributes of a Good Theory. . . .119
Classification 120
Components 115
Conceptual Frameworks. 125
Defined 111
Goal or Purpose of Theory. 118
Theory and Research
Framework. 130
V
Validity and Reliability 230